"I first met Tor a privilege and a wonderful lear him, particularly through sport peak physical fitness, mental toughness, and inner motivation are all-important. Tony not only brings huge energy and enthusiasm to his specialized area of work, but also vast knowledge and insight as how the body and mind work. Tony's genius is that he has translated this knowledge into an easy-to-understand and applied approach which allows us to be the very best we can be in our chosen field and in our aspirations and goals."

Michael Ostinelli

Director

Community, Education & Voluntary Sector

The Pacific Institute Ireland

***

"I have been working with Tony for the past 3 months. Since starting this program, my flexibility has improved dramatically, and I have remained injury free. I combine his workout program with my own gym work and find they go very well together. The extra core strength and total body awareness that I now have, helps me get more out of every workout."

Brian

"I asked Tony to help out with a female adult sports team I was coaching regarding some strength and conditioning work 6 to 7 weeks before our playoffs begun. The group is made up of mixed ability players and after 5 weeks of the program their conditioning had improved dramatically. By boosting their confidence through improved fitness levels and skill levels they also showed major improvements with their mental strength capacity. He has done this by his great communication skills and his vast knowledge. I would recommend him to any sporting organization at whatever standard your team is at. Thanks Tony."

Coach Mike

***

"After the birth of my third child I found it hard to lose some unwanted post baby weight. I started training with Tony in his Pilates class, and with his guidance I started running not long after that. I have been using his program ever since. I am now running marathon distances comfortably. His program provides me with all the daily energy and vitality I need to look after 3 young children and stay in great shape."

Leah

"I have been incorporating Tony's exercise program into both my athletic and gym workouts for the past 18 months and find it a great addition to both. The increase in my flexibility, core strength, and power has been very noticeable. It has helped me reduce my incidences of injury and has helped me make big sporting gains by training smarter. I would highly recommend using this program to help you get the most out of your chosen exercise routine - whatever it may be."

Dave

***

"As my children started to get a little older I decided to focus on one of my own personal goals-Running a Marathon. I am delighted to say that goal was achieved within 10 months of starting my training. Tony's Quantum Flow Running Program was instrumental in keeping me injury and pain free for the duration of my training. This training system allowed me to enjoy the full training program and gave me back a strong, toned, athletic body that I thought was long gone. I now use some of his techniques with my children to help them move and feel better in their sports."

Tanya

QUANTUM FLOW RUNNING

How to train smarter, prevent injury, and
get the most from your exercise routine

TONY LAWLESS

Health & Wellness Educator

QUANTUMFLOW
PERFORMANCE

Published by Quantum Flo Ltd.

Dublin, Ireland

Cover by Una Healy/Una Healy Design

Photography by Monika Foltman

Fonts used: Book Antiqua and Arial, with permission from Microsoft.

ISBN-13: 978-1-5272-2486-5

DEDICATION

For Lisa, Jennifer, and Matthew

I am eternally grateful for your ongoing support in my work and for your love in my life.

CONTENTS

LETTER FROM TONY LAWLESS

I am delighted to be able to share with you the holistic health techniques that I have learned over the past 25 years which have brought me much happiness and success. I feel that if we can all start to regain our independence and self-confidence and reconnect to our true self, we will make this world a better place for ourselves as well as many others. I can honestly say that running has played a major part in helping me to lead a happy and fulfilled life. Even when I was growing up I can remember my Mum tactfully suggesting to me to "go for a run" if my mood was less than agreeable. I always went because we both knew that by the time I would get back from my run I would be "Happy Tony" again.

This sort of journey can only start with yourself and your personal health and well-being. Cultivating the gift of emotional self-sufficiency should be everyone's long-term goal. I sincerely wish you every success along your path to total health and wellness. I hope this book will inspire you to live a healthier, happier, and more rewarding life... The life you deserve.

Tony Lawless

70% of the proceeds of this limited-edition launch copy of Quantum Flow Running will be going to support the work of Pieta House, the Centre for the Prevention of Suicide and Self-Harm. Since 2006, Pieta House has been providing its free counselling services to people in suicidal distress and people engaging in self-harm. In 2016, the service expanded to include a 24-hour helpline as well as suicide bereavement counselling, and to date has provided therapy for over 30,000 clients across Ireland.

FOREWORD

Modern life presents a number of challenges to our physical health. We are becoming increasingly busier at home and at work with pressure and expectations of the modern world. Paradoxically, we have also become increasingly sedentary and associated dietary changes have resulted in epidemics of heart disease, obesity, and diabetes. Hours spent commuting while sitting in cars, trains, and buses, followed by protracted time in front of computers and television screens lead to chronic back pain and reduced fitness. Advances in medicine and nutrition mean we can expect to live longer; but the quality of the added years is diminished by chronic medical conditions, increased frailty, and dependency in old age.

It is widely agreed that physical activity coupled with a good diet is the key to the prevention of many chronic degenerative conditions and the maintenance of health. Numerous studies have proven the benefits of exercise performed for as little as thirty minutes for four times a week. However, too often people take on new resolutions to begin or increase their exercise without careful preparation. The result can be injury, frustration, failure to reach goals, and therefore, a reluctance to re-engage.

In this book Tony sets about giving readers the tools to take action to improve their overall physical and mental health. With his extensive experience in the field and holistic approach, Tony describes the importance of a methodical approach to improving and maintaining fitness without injury and achieving new personal bests and goals previously elusive. The cornerstone of his approach is the building of flexibility, stability, and strength using simple exercises which boost potential and performance. In essence, his exercises teach us to perform better and with less effort. To further optimize the body's fitness, he coaches us on careful hydration, a logical approach to nutrition and breathing techniques which increase overall vitality and enhance the ability of the body to repair itself.

Whether you're an Olympic athlete or a newcomer to exercise, this book is an excellent motivating companion guide to a more thoughtful and active life. It provides a methodical approach to all physical exercise and training to enable the reader to stay injury free and achieve more than they ever thought possible.

Professor Sean Gaine

Chief Medical Officer

Olympic Council of Ireland

Athens | Beijing | London | Rio

INTRODUCTION

Whether you are just starting to discover the joy of running or you are a seasoned exerciser, there is plenty of information in this book. Quantum Flow Running is an easy to follow, smart program that will teach you a new way to approach running by using an efficient Total Body Warm Up, Stability, and Recovery Program. It will enable you to get the maximum benefit from every training session by developing the elasticity and strength of muscle groups that are vital for peak performance. It will also provide you with a clear understanding of how key organs function in your body, along with the obvious benefits available to you when you improve their daily functionality.

Over the years I have listened to many clients talk about how hard they find training and have witnessed the negative effects that incorrect training methods have taken on their bodies. Every sport involves movement, and this program is the key to enhancing your ability to move in a smoother way. Why is this important? Because smooth movement is more efficient and efficient movement generates less negative stress on your joints and on the body as a whole. In essence, you will perform better and with less effort.

Many sports books and Apps available on the market only focus on training routines that build muscle and strength.

There are very few exercise programs that understand and address the deep critical need for all aspects of a body to repair after a training session. There is a deeper level of body conditioning that needs to take place in order for optimum energy to be created and harnessed. That deeper level comes from a total body or "holistic" approach to training.

We all stand, walk, run, and move in a slightly different way, and that's OK. I don't want to force you to change how you move or your running style. I want to give you techniques to help you bring symmetry and strength into your body while helping you to stay injury free. The goal of this book is to help make your daily physical movements and workout sessions as comfortable and as enjoyable as possible, so you can exercise in a way that brings energy, relaxation, and reward into your life, rather than leaving you tired and sore. It gives you the power to take control of your body, know how it works, and how it moves for you while introducing you to an understanding of what is required to achieve optimum health.

Many people are only aware of how their muscles look and feel from the outside; and therefore, only train what they can see. Quantum Flow Running trains and improves not only the muscle but also the fascia and the organ functions of the body. It works on 3 different levels. By focusing on these three systems simultaneously, you are facilitating and encouraging a deeper and more complete form of Health, Fitness, and Vitality. Think of this as a 3-Dimensional approach to movement that is sure to give you an edge and help you achieve your full potential with no extra training time required.

An intelligent training system should build equal amounts of strength and flexibility to develop elasticity in muscles. Elasticity = Power.

Once your body is flexible and cleared out of toxins, it's time to nourish it. As well as creating these exercise routines to help you get stronger and faster, I have also created a range of

Nutrition Supplements that are designed to help you meet your extra energy and recovery needs. The supplements are high quality, and rather than focusing on just specific individual elements, I have focused on ingredients that improve critical full body functions. For example, the two supplements that I would recommend to active people are "All Day Energy" and "SportsMax." Improved sustainable energy levels and faster recovery times are what most sports people who lead a busy life want. These two products are perfect for people who like to pack a lot of action into everyday life.

My pre-training product "SportsMax," has been formulated to take advantage of the findings of the 1998 Medical Nobel Prize Winner, Dr. Louis Ignore. "SportsMax" may also assist you in stabilizing your blood pressure and lower cholesterol levels if taken on a daily basis. It is, in essence, a full cardiovascular supplement which will help greatly with circulation. At the same time, and as a result of improved circulation, it can greatly increase energy levels which improve sports performance. "SportsMax" also delivers a high level of nutrition to help speed up your post-workout recovery and repair.

"All Day Energy" is made from just one ingredient- pure Irish Oysters. They are packed full of nutritional goodness and provide a steady smooth energy boost that will last the whole day and well into the evening with no negative side effects in relation to sleep and relaxation.

WHY QUANTUM FLOW RUNNING WORKS

The primary reason for using this holistic running program is to improve the amount of elasticity in your muscles, to improve your oxygen efficiency, your blood quality, and learn how to work in harmony with yourself. By improving the elasticity in your muscles, you can improve the power-to-weight ratio in your body, making you able to run faster and smoother. More elasticity also greatly lessens the risk of injury.

Secondly, it is important to improve your fuel supply systems, namely oxygen, and nutrition. Your overall health is largely dictated by the quality of your blood, and that's why blood testing in hospitals is so widely used. If your blood is not as clean as it could be, then your body will not be able to transport these two most important elements around your body efficiently. Applying the smart nutrition principles in Part 4 is how we go about achieving that. We do this by introducing the concept of cleaning your system through detoxification methods specifically to cater to your body's needs, that will ensure optimum nutrition through targeted supplements and foods that alkalize the body.

Developing your core muscles will help you perform daily tasks with less effort, making more energy available for you during your workout.

Quantum Flow Running is different from ordinary running because it insists on connecting your onboard computer (your brain) with your body before you take to the road. You will learn to listen and act on what subtle signals you are being sent by your body and become pro-active rather than re-active. All these components combined will lead you to run in a balanced state, and it is this state of correct body balance that will allow you to enjoy this great sport for many years to come.

This may sound simple and in reality, it is. But like anything new you try, it can take a little getting used to. So, what I have done in this book to help you implement the system faster is break the transition period of reconnection between your mind and body into a simple step-by-step plan for you to follow. I take you through the main components in your body that when improved; individually will provide you with a strong, flexible, and an even more energized body and mind.

Lifestyle can do a number on you. Let's talk about stress, shall we? You are in your early forties; you have family and work responsibilities. You don't have a moment to yourself. Aches and pains have become a regular part of your life, and then there's the tiredness. Can you relate?

Quantum Flow Running works because it supports the whole body and mind, but also... and this is crucial, it does it efficiently. Taking these small smart steps that I advocate in this program will bring you the maximum results for the minimum effort. Am I saying no effort... no, I am not. But efficiency is something to be prized.

WHO IS QUANTUM FLOW RUNNING FOR?

Quantum Flow Running is for a range of people that includes the following:

For first time runners who are starting their running journey a little later in life. Juggling a heavy workload in college, marriage, children, and (or) a career can all contribute to a late start in the running craze. Except it's not a craze anymore. Year on year running is the fastest growing leisure activity in the USA. In fact, according to a nationwide report, figures have grown steadily since the mid-90s to a staggering 18,023,000, and that's just the figures for people between the ages of 25-44. The massive continuous growth in this sport should lead you to the mindset that if so many others are doing this, so can I. So, if you are looking for a safe and smart way to avoid injury and enjoy the health benefits that regular running can deliver, please read on.

Those who are at the very start of a running goal will find important advice on how to safely get started and take the first steps towards that goal. In my practice, I have found beginners are most likely to get injured or just give up before they have time to build the momentum required to keep coming back session after session; and start to enjoy the long-term health benefits that running regularly delivers over time.

If this is you, my first piece of advice for you is to join a running club or at least a group of like-minded people who will be willing to share their running stories and training tips with you. They will also know all the best local running routes to take and which will be suitable for you and more importantly which ones to avoid.

In many ways when you start to run you also start on a journey of self-discovery. You will be asked to identify and overcome areas of both physical and mental discomfort which you may not have even been aware of in the past. With the help of some running buddies and this book, you will be better equipped to overcome those challenges both in the short and long-term. The main thing is to get organized, get informed, and get moving.

This book is also suitable for runners who are still in the early stages of their running career in experience terms as opposed to age terms and have realized that they are now ready to move forward to the next level. (Once you have discovered the freedom of running and are used to about 3 times for 20 minutes on average per week, you will most likely want to move to the next level).

Increasing your weekly running distance will also introduce some new challenges to your workouts. It can cause increased levels of soreness; and therefore, you will need to invest more time in your Recovery process. Nutrition will also play an increasingly bigger part in the success of your training routine. As your body becomes leaner, you will need to change your mindset and view food as fuel for your body. This is the time to move away from the sugary treats and snacks that you may have been partial to in the past. There are some great sports nutrition books available, but because many people have different likes and dislike around certain food types, I have decided to just present enough dietary information to give you basic, easy to follow guidelines to get you through this phase until you have time to reach deeper into this topic.

Then there are those who have moved past the 5k / 10k park run and are now working towards the ½ marathons and full marathon distance. While you now have a good idea of the many components that make up a strong progressive running schedule, the added value of an efficient warm up, stability, and recovery program which is possible to adapt into an already established training plan is invaluable.

Runners face a whole new set of challenges when they decide to take on a marathon training program. As weekly mileage starts to go up and the countdown to the start line looms, you can be tempted to run through injuries. The closer you get to the starting line, the more inclined your training schedule and body become to implode under the high mileage you have been covering over the previous months. When I found myself with just 6 weeks to train for my first marathon, I made sure to focus on my recovery protocol between my sessions.

The key to successfully move up to this level is to build elasticity into the muscles. This is done through increasing your current levels of flexibility and stability, which will lead to a better power-to-weight ratio for you. It will not only help you to run faster but also lessen your risk of injury and believe me; you can't afford 4 weeks off of training for a marathon to rehab an injury that you could have avoided.

If you are already at the top of your career and are totally satisfied with your performance, then I would recommend you stick to what you are doing and enjoy every minute of every run - you deserve it. Having said that, you may like to check out my range of quality nutrition supplements at:

www.QuantumFlowPerformance.com/

There are also many other interesting training tips discussed in the book which has their origins in almost 20 years of my holistic health and Pilates practice. It is these insights into how the body works and how best to harness the massive benefits that running on a regular basis can deliver to you that makes me think that you will find something in this book that is missing from many others.

The Quantum Flow philosophy is all about living and moving along on the path of least resistance.

WHAT DOES IT NOT DO?

This book will help you efficiently prepare for and repair from training sessions. It is not; however, designed to take the place of a cardiovascular workout. I would recommend getting up to 30 minutes of cardio exercise 3 times per week.

Also, if you are not currently at this standard, then I would recommend that you seek a local qualified personal trainer who will construct a safe plan for you to follow. He/she will be able to help you develop a suitable exercise program to help you achieve your health and fitness goals.

Remember the goal of the information in this book is to improve your health and energy levels safely. So, if you feel you are not quite up to this standard yet you need to follow a smart safe protocol before you start exercising. Talk to your doctor and make sure you follow his/her recommendations

HOW TO USE THIS BOOK

You get to decide how you use this book. Keep in mind that cutting corners is not the best way to go about this especially since the whole purpose of the book is for you to enjoy injury free running. If you are just starting, then I recommend going through the whole program. If you are adding aspects of this to an existing program, by all means, pick and choose.

The full sequence is as follows:

1. You introduce some key steps to enhance or create your running program.
2. You focus on getting flexible first. Perform all the exercises daily. There are just three sets of simple exercises for you to follow that need almost no equipment and very little space. So, no matter where you live or what your lifestyle is, you will be able to use this system and benefit from them.
3. You add breathing exercises to expand your lung capacity; and therefore, your bodies access to oxygen... running fuel.
4. You learn about running form. Correct foot placement and strengthening exercises will help you avoid injury and increase your speed.
5. You focus on diet. Consuming correct foods and supplements will reduce inflammation and improve your daily energy levels.
6. You detox and nourish your workhorse organs (heart, lungs, liver, and kidneys).

7. You set realistic manageable fitness/lifestyle goals.
8. You partner up with someone for mutual support or join a club. The camaraderie of going on the same journey can be great fun and hugely supportive when you have one of those days. We've all had them...

QUICK START

You can use the Quick Start 28 Day Running Plan (Appendix I) to get going if you don't have an existing running schedule. It shows how to incorporate the warm up, stability, and recovery exercises.

It contains the least amount of information to get you up and running safely. Work through these few pages diligently, take your time, and make sure you understand all the relevant information. It is important that you pay close attention to detail and make sure each move is performed with accuracy and integrity. Only then, is when you should feel confident to start using the program.

Make sure to slow down the moves and focus on one at a time. Be patient, get to know the moves not just mentally, but also give your body time to grow into the sequence of exercises.

If you are an unexperienced runner, you will still need to go through each exercise a couple of times slowly before you become comfortable with the flow of the full routine. If you are a more experienced runner, I would advise you to use the quick start guide as a checklist. This way you are still refreshing already learned knowledge, and who knows- you may even learn something new and important that you can bring into your weekly training routine.

I have deliberately tried to keep the information in this book to a minimum in order to make sure you finish it and act on the principles discussed within. It is designed to encourage action. To get you out of your chair and put the key principles of this modern 3D approach to movement and running into action.

All I ask is that you can commit 15 minutes of your workout time to incorporate the Quantum Flow Program into your routine. You will see great improvements as you become more and more familiar with the exercises. And you will simply absorb them into your workout with no extra time needed. Like everything in life, it's what you do on a regular basis that brings the best results.

Depending on your current level of fitness you should experience positive results by the end of week three.

So, now that you have decided to act on your instinct and avail yourself of this Quantum Flow Running 3D training program, let's not waste any time. It's time to get started!

"Action leads to motivation and focused motivation leads to successful outcomes."

Tony Lawless

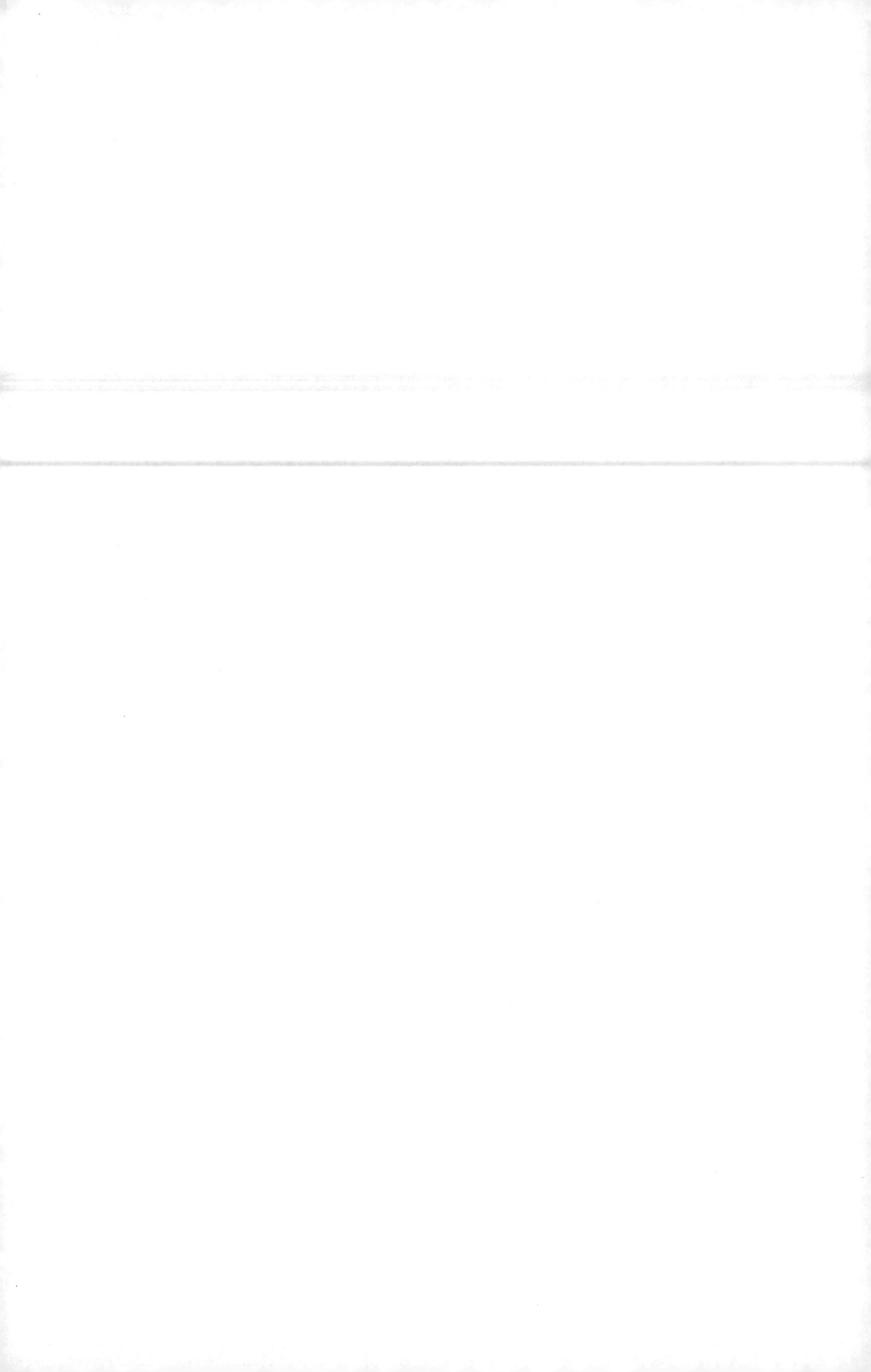

PART 1: GETTING STARTED

1: GETTING STARTED

We may all be at different stages of our life, but there are two things that we all desire and benefit from because they make living a lot easier and more fun. They are- our need for plenty of energy and a good level of mobility. When most people start running for the first time they talk about how hard it is for them to catch their breath and sustain the pace. It is very easy to give up after just one or two sessions when in fact these first sessions are the absolute hardest of all and everything after them gets easier.

As a beginner, you need to stick to a simple plan that will support you through the tough starting phase and protect you from injury. My advice to all beginners is to start gently, push your work rate up to about 75% of what you feel is possible, and set each workout session up to give you the best possible chance to succeed and enjoy the experience. In other words– finish your session strong with the attitude that "I can do more, or I am able to do more" rather than saying "I am not able to do this." This simple mind shift will help keep your confidence levels high while keeping you safe at a time when you are vulnerable and need all the help and encouragement to keep going. In essence, you are learning to become your own personal coach. The sense of independence, confidence, and personal satisfaction that accompanies the ability to be your own coach will then give you the ability to motivate yourself during your more challenging training sessions. This mindset will then overflow into your personal life too.

If you are brand new to running, the best way for you to use this book is to go to the Self-Assessment section and go through the 13 questions I have set out for you. By taking the time to answer these questions and analyzing your scores, you will give yourself an automatic awareness of how you are physically and how confident you are in your ability.

It's important to gain a realistic frame of mind at this stage because you may be feeling excited at the prospect of starting a new challenge and overlook the reality that progress for the first month will probably be slower than you hoped. It is vital that you establish a clear starting point and use this first Self-Assessment to track your progress rather than just making unreasonable assumptions about your progress. Most people substantially overestimate what they can achieve in a short period and substantially underestimate what they can achieve over a longer period. So, start from the beginning, go slowly, and learn to be your own source of personal motivation- more on how to become your own source of positivity later.

If you have been running for more than six months, you will hopefully be starting to feel all the benefits that regular running has to offer. You should be starting to hit some of your early goals. Your body shape will be starting to change, and your confidence levels should be strong. At this stage of a running program it is easy for an athlete to become complacent and assume that they know everything and start to cut corners. The two most obvious areas that people start to cut corners on are the Warm up and the Recovery phases. If the tendency is for you to skip these parts of your training program, then it is likely that you will pick up some sort of injury along the way. By always warming up correctly and using the system in this book correctly, you will be able to identify if there are any sore areas (muscles / joints) in your body before you start your workout. You can then take care not to over-train the area and focus more recovery techniques on the specific sore or tight areas.

If you are in this category, then I would ask you to slow down, take the time to go through the Self-Assessment form, and see how you are currently rating yourself. You should then take time to ponder just how far you have come and make sure that your progress is well noted. This will serve two purposes for you. First, you will be able to see just how far you have come since you started. Second, you will now have a baseline to track your progress with.

For those of you who have been running for a number of years it is possible to hit a plateau. If you don't recognize you are currently on a plateau, it is impossible for you to overcome it quickly. By using the Self-Assessment form, you will quickly get an idea of exactly where you are both mentally and physically. It will also tell you where your strengths and weaknesses are. Clarity will bring you renewed focus, and you can freshen up your workouts with a new routine. This should help to get you out of your plateau and back on track. You may even realize that you are over-training and under-recovering. If the recovery system you are using is not sufficient, then you are going to be heading towards either a performance flat line or negative curve in the long run, instead of moving forward and making good improvements. Take the time to go back to the basics and reinvigorate your training schedule in order to jump forward to the next level without having to commit any extra time to your workouts.

2: SELF-ASSESSMENT

This is where we start by looking at our baseline. These assessment questions and the flexibility exercises will set the journey you will take. Like everyone, there will be areas where you excel and areas where you need room for improvement. Later in the chapter I provide a list of activities to help you progress in the areas that need improving. The idea is that you will regularly return to the assessment section to track your progress. I have chosen some meaningful categories which will reveal much about your overall wellness at a glance.

So just take a few minutes right now to rate yourself on a scale of 1 to 9 for each of these categories.

(1 = poor; 3 = fair; 5 = average; 7 = good; 9 = excellent)

SLEEP QUALITY

1 = Less than 3 hours of broken sleep most nights,

9 = 6-8 hours of sleep per night

RESISTANCE TO ILLNESS

1 = Sick regularly; 9 = Not sick in the last 5 years

TRAINING KNOWLEDGE

1 = Never trained before; 9 = Have worked with a personal trainer regularly, understand my dietary needs and enjoy training

PAST DEDICATION TO TRAINING

1 = Never done any training; 9 = train 3 to 5 times per week

DAILY MOTIVATION LEVELS

1 = Just get on with life; 9 = I love following a new plan that makes me feel better

NUTRITIONAL KNOWLEDGE

1 = I eat whatever and whenever I feel like; 9 = Enjoy healthy food and make the right choice 90% of the time

OVERALL HEALTH

1 = Tired; stiff and sore; 9 = Fit and well

BODY MOBILITY | FLEXIBILITY

1 = Find it hard to get up out of a chair or can't touch my shins; 9 = Can place my hands flat on the ground while my legs are straight and have no mobility issues

MUSCLE AND JOINT PAIN

1 = lots; 9 = none

BODY COMPOSITION

1 = Unacceptably flabby; 9 = Very lean

BODY WEIGHT

1 = Very far from your target weight; 9 = Right at your target weight

STRENGTH

1 = Just standing makes me tired; 9 = Can comfortably perform extra tasks daily

ENDURANCE

1 = A short walk leaves me out of breath; 9 = Happy to put in a big training session after a busy day at work

FLEXIBILITY ASSESSMENT

Now complete these simple flexibility exercises and also rate your score from 1 to 9 in the same manner as above.

What you are testing is how far you can reach and if you feel a very obvious tension pain in the area below the knees during the stretches. You want to be able to reach further with less pain every time you retake the test. You are just looking for a continuous improvement- being able to reach the floor with no pain would be ranked 9 while reaching to just below your knees would be ranked 1.

The best way to help release the tension from the lower legs is to use a spikey ball or tennis ball under the soles of the feet.

With 2 straight legs bend forward from your hips (fig 201), let your arms hang softly towards the ground. Hold for 8 seconds and assess your range of flexibility.

fig 201

Now bend one leg at the knee and keep the other straight (fig 202). Reach towards your toes. Hold for 8 seconds and assess your range of flexibility. Then repeat on the other leg.

fig 202

Turn your toes to face inward as much as possible (fig 203) and repeat the flexibility test above.

fig 203

Now turn your feet as far out as you possibly can and repeat the flexibility test above (fig 204).

fig 204

These 4 simple tests should give you an idea of what areas of your legs are tight. This test should be performed every two weeks to keep an eye on hip and leg function.

Improving continually is as close to perfection as anyone can get. Enjoy every training session.

HOW TO READ THE RESULTS

It is most important that you realize that the hardest steps to take towards any goal are the first few. Congratulations- you have just done that. Constructing a baseline or starting point is all about gaining clarity. Because you will have to undergo this assessment regularly, you will also have some personal accountability. Now it's about getting a plan together that you can stick to and moving towards a healthier, happier you. I have no doubt that you will start to feel better once you take ownership of your future and invest some time into making the adjustments needed to give you more energy. A rise in energy will cause a spike in self-belief, and when you combine those two elements together your performance levels go up dramatically.

BELOW 40

If your score is below 40, then I would suggest that you seek a personal trainer who will help provide you with the initial motivation and support that you may benefit from as well as the local information of other services that you may need to consult in order for you to succeed.

BETWEEN 41–60

If you are just starting out and filling in the Self-Assessment form for the first time, you may have realized that your health and energy levels are not all they could be. There are several reasons why your score may be at this level. Nutrition and exercise are the two main reasons why you may have scored in this low to mid-range. They affect the efficiency of almost every system in our body, and if we are clogged up with toxins floating around our body, it becomes very difficult for us to eliminate waste and to transport fresh nutrition into our cells. We become tired easily and lose motivation very quickly. We need to clean out the toxins that build up in us daily and make a big effort to keep our circulation at its optimum level; this can be hard, especially as we get older. By focusing on quality nutrition i.e. substituting fruit for sugar and caffeine, fiber for some carbs, and proteins for saturated fats, you should be able to restore some balance back in your food intake. You will also see an improvement in your energy levels and an improvement in your moods. Once you identify where your current routine is holding you back it is easy to make some positive changes and track your progress in your training diary.

BETWEEN 61-80

If your final numbers are between 61-80 you are definitely on the right track. You are already well on the way to living a healthy lifestyle. You are probably keen to take your energy and performance to the next level, and the key to doing this is to use the charts provided to track your performance. Many of us do not have a training partner or an accountability buddy, and even if you do have someone to help you stay on the right track, it is best you become self-accountable. Self-sufficiency and self-analysis is the key to personal development, not just in fitness, but in life.

You should use the Self-Assessment forms weekly to track and identify where your strong and weak points are and set weekly targets to help you improve on every aspect of your routine.

ABOVE 81

Well done. If you have scored yourself at this level, then you should be very proud of this achievement. There are just a couple of questions I need you to answer honestly. The first one is: Is this level of living sustainable for you? Does it feel right for you, or is it a struggle?

And my second question to you is: Is your life in balance? Are you over obsessed with the physical and missing out on emotional connections as a result?

The whole idea of this running program is to make your training as efficient as possible but also to help you use the benefits that you gain from every workout in living a healthy and content life. The goal is always to stay in balance and by filling out this Self-Assessment form regularly you will be able to make sure you stay on track and do not become over obsessed with any training program.

ONGOING IMPROVEMENT GUIDELINES

Now that you know your baseline in the different categories you can work on the areas that need improving one day at a time.

OVERALL HEALTH

If you have endured a health issue or are currently on medication and under medical supervision, I would advise you to talk to your doctor before you start taking any exercise.

1. Go gently.
2. Stop if you are feeling light-headed or notice chest pains.
3. Take into consideration your current weight, age, and fitness level.
4. The safest way to exercise on your own when starting a new program is to make sure the training sessions give you energy and leave you looking forward to your next session.

Keep an eye on your heart rate. The best way to make sure you are not overexerting is to stay within the training zone and to understand which end of the zone you need to be in. See the **Target Heart Zone Chart** on page 29, for a quick reference guide that will help you find your target training zone.

When training in the "fat burning" zone, (i.e. longer runs), it is best to stay within the Target Heart Rate Zone. This is usually described as 60% of your maximum heart rate. This is because you will be able to train for longer; and therefore, burn more calories while improving your stamina. A good reference point is to check that you can carry out a steady conversation while running in the fat burning zone. If you find yourself unable to talk smoothly, then you are more than likely over stressing your heart. If you are looking to improve speed and are focused on doing a speed session, then you will run much shorter distances at a faster pace. The threshold zone for this type of training is said to be between 80-90% of your maximum heart rate. This type of training session will lead to dramatic increases in heart rate very quickly and the numbers on the Average Maximum Heart Rate Scale will be your guideline.

If you are just starting out, please be smart; keep a close eye on your heart numbers. Always stay on the lower side of the numbers suggested in the table.

Some days you will feel stronger than others and if you only check your times when you first start your training sessions, you are likely to over-stress at some point. When you are tired, your heart will not be able to produce as much exertion as when you are well rested. Therefore, when you track your heart rate during your training sessions, you make sure that you are training smarter.

Use this formula to make sure you do not exceed your "average maximum heart rate" while training. Subtract your age from 220 to keep you safe.

Example: 43 years old: 220 - 43 = 177. Therefore, if this person's heart rate goes above 177 beats per minute, they are running the risk of overloading the heart and need to slow down or stop until the heart rate comes back within the suggested limits.

TARGET HEART ZONE CHART

Age	Target HR Zone 50-85%	Average Maximum Heart Rate, 100%
20	100 - 170 beats per minute	200 beats per minute
30	95 - 162 beats per minute	190 beats per minute
35	93 - 157 beats per minute	185 beats per minute
40	90 - 153 beats per minute	180 beats per minute
45	87 - 148 beats per minute	175 beats per minute
50	83 – 144 beats per minute	170 beats per minute
55	78 – 139 beats per minute	165 beats per minute

Remember, the chart is only offered as a quick reference training guideline.

MANUAL HEART RATE CHECK

If you do not train with a heart rate monitor, you can use this simple technique to make sure you are staying within your safe training zone.

1. Stop running.

2. To check your pulse - rotate the palm of your left hand to face upward. Now bend your left wrist 10% so that your fingers are facing upward. Place the 3 middle fingers on your right hand just above the center point and to the outside of your left wrist. Press in at that point and your middle finger should be able to locate your pulse

3. Take your pulse for 15 seconds…

4. Multiply this number by 4 to calculate your beats per minute.

HOW TO FIND YOUR RECOVERY HEART RATE

1. You should first take your resting pulse and record your number. It is best to do this first thing in the morning.

2. Then take your pulse rate straight after exercising. Record your number.

3. Then take your pulse rate one minute later. Record your number.

4. Subtract the number for the second pulse rate from the first pulse rate after exercise.

5. This is the recovery heart rate number.

IMPROVING ASSESSMENT RESULTS

TRAINING KNOWLEDGE

1. Start listening to your body. If you have trained hard recently and your muscles are still sore or stiff from your last workout or race, you should be aware of what your body is trying to tell you. Focus on your recovery at this point rather than trying to push through the pain. If you push beyond your limits, you will end up injured or at the very least find yourself stuck on a training plateau.

2. Change your "one-size-fits-all" approach. No matter what routine or training system you are currently following there is always room to refine and improve it. The one-size-fits-all approach is fine for getting started, but you should view every training program as a detailed guideline only.

3. The Quantum Flow approach is designed to help you identify specific personal weaknesses in your own mobility and flexibility. It uses exercises to improve the function of your weaker areas. When you go through the full exercise routine, you will identify those parts that you need to work on and instead of just working on one individual area or muscle the Quantum Flow routine works to re-balance the whole body. That is why it is known as a holistic approach. Lack of mobility is the biggest cause of injury, and in order to restore correct levels of mobility you should always address the full body rather than just focusing on one specific area.

4. Read reliable online information. One of the most obvious and best ways to improve your training knowledge is to read. There are plenty of online information sites pushing out volumes of content, but most of it is for advertising. Move away from all the

clutter and try to find just a couple of reliable information sources that are relevant to your current level.

5. Running magazines and online forums are always a great source of knowledge. Always take time when introducing something new into your routine. The first couple of times you try something new you should adapt the mindset "I am going to stay within my limits." Get to know the exercise and make sure to leave the new exercise thinking that you can do better the next time; that way you won't over stretch yourself and do damage.

6. Experiment. Try new techniques that you feel will enhance your training program. Always start a new technique by paying very close attention to the precise movements involved. Watch the move a few times, then perform the move slowly and see if you can feel which part of your body the exercise is targeting. When you start a new exercise, the temptation is to over-do the exercise due to the novelty and excitement of trying something new. It is best to go slow and leave yourself wanting more. There is a good chance that if you over-do a new exercise, there will be soreness the next day in unexpected areas.

7. Self-Assess. By taking this self-assessment test on a monthly basis you will become more aware of how your body responds to the training you are doing, and that is a great way to improve your training knowledge. You will learn what works for you and more importantly what doesn't. Refining your training program is the quickest way to self-sufficiency and the achievement of your goals.

PAST DEDICATION TO TRAINING

If your dedication to training in the past has not been successful, you should take a few minutes to answer the 5 questions below and explore why it was not sustainable for you long-term.

1. Did the type of exercises or training programs you were involved in suit your needs and match your goals?
2. Why was it not sustainable? Did you not enjoy it?
3. Was it too intense for you?
4. What have you learned from your past training routine experiences?
5. How can you make this program work for you?

DAILY MOTIVATION LEVELS

Motivation is directly linked to energy. The more energy you have the more motivated you will feel to get something done. These are my tips to help you stay motivated.

1. Drink a lot of water and stay well hydrated.
2. Pay close attention to your diet especially your snacks between meals as we are most likely to go astray with our snacks.
3. Get plenty of sleep. About seven hours per night is a good guideline.
4. Use a journal to track your progress.
5. Get organized early. Schedule your training times well in advance and make sure you have the necessary gear ready for the relevant weather conditions.

Nutrition Knowledge

As with your training knowledge, your nutritional knowledge is also very important.

1. You should look for impartial advice from government agencies to improve your basic understanding of nutrition. The best way to make sure you are getting impartial knowledge is to see if the article you are reading is not advertising something. If there is no advertising linked in the article, then you will usually find it is worth considering. But always be careful to analyze the information to see if it applies to you. Alternatively, you could take an online course or even make an appointment to see a practicing sports nutritionist.

2. Know that everyone is different and has different needs / likes and dislikes.

3. Eating large meals late in the evening is a bad idea.

4. Fresh home cooked food is your best chance of avoiding high calorie foods.

5. Raw foods like fresh fruit and vegetables are great options.

Body Mobility and Flexibility

There can be any number of reasons why you can have poor mobility and flexibility. These are my tips to help you improve your flexibility.

1. Warm up well before conducting any exercise

2. Make sure to do a good cool down after every workout

3. Eat good quality sources of protein to help repair sore/stiff muscles.

4. Stretch daily and pay attention to your hips and lower back

5. Be aware that emotional stress can lead to a reduction in mobility. So, if you have had "a bad day" you may not be able to train at your optimum level straight away. Just ease into the workout and then see how you feel after about 30 minutes. Exercise dissolves stress.

MUSCLE AND JOINT PAIN

Muscle and joint pain will vary for most people. How you treat the pain is completely linked to how you got the pain in the first place.

1. A simple strain or light swelling may take a couple of days rest and regular applications of ice to get you back running.

2. If you still can't walk comfortably after six days, it's time to get an assessment from a physio or neuromuscular therapist.

3. Muscle pain can arise from over-training or just a tough workout and a couple of days off will sort that out.

4. If you suffer from joint pain, I would recommend a joint care supplement which contains glucosamine.

5. A lot of runners suffer from issues in their knees and inflammation around the kneecap is very common. This can be caused by a tight Psoas muscle, but because the kneecap is only one of two floating bones (not attached to another bone) in your body, it is very susceptible to misalignment especially if there are issues higher up in the hip region.

Body Weight

1. You can check the online guidelines for correct weight in relation to your height.

1. Because this may be the starting point of your running journey or a new approach to running there is a good chance you are at least a little off your target weight. But again, it's all about getting a starting point and logging the progress.

2. When you combine the correct food and nutrition with exercise, you can make massive progress towards achieving what you perceive to be your optimum weight.

Body Composition

This part of the assessment form is to help you get a realistic idea of where you are right now. Honesty will bring clarity and focus.

1. You need to be very realistic with your assessment as well as your expectations. Remember I am not asking you to judge yourself here. The reason you are doing this exercise is to give you a baseline or starting point. Once you make a starting assessment- then you can clearly track progress. I find that many people do not see themselves as they are and can often have an incorrect perception of themselves. If you have a partner or close friend, it might help to ask them for an honest opinion.

2. The fact that you have already taken action by purchasing this book and are reading it, tells me that you are ready to either start a new health or fitness stage in your life or find a way to get more out of your current fitness plan. Either way, it's the first step forward and rather than getting hung up on the results that the system can provide you are advised to just trust the

process. Show up, do the work to the best of your ability and reap the rewards as they arrive.

3. You must be prepared for delayed gratification. Sow the exercise seed now and reap the rewards later.

4. If this is a starting point for a new health and fitness regime and it has been a while since you exercised, progress may be slow to start with and most people give up too early just because they can't achieve immediate results. It takes time to activate hormones, and I always recommend allowing about 6 weeks of regular exercise to give your metabolism a chance to ignite and start shedding noticeable weight. Initially, the body will balance any fluid retention issues that may be present. Then it will start to gain some internal/external flexibility and strength. Once correct eating habits are adhered to, the body will start to burn fat, the appetite will shift away from sugar cravings towards proteins, and the sequence will start all over again.

5. If you have been exercising for a while and you are looking to move your routine up to the next level, you should already have a clear picture of where your strong and weak points are in relation to body composition. Most people find the mid-section or tummy area could use extra attention and if you focus on using the stability section of this program regularly, you should see good results within about 16 sessions. The most important part of the stability exercises is to focus on maintaining correct core connection for the full duration of every set of exercises.

Sleep Patterns

1. Stick to a sleep schedule. Whenever possible go to bed as near to or the same time as possible every night and get up at the same time every morning, even on weekends. A consistent routine reinforces your body's

sleep-wake cycle. If you find that you don't fall asleep within about 20 minutes, get up and do something relaxing and then go back to bed when you're tired.

2. Play it cool. It is better to sleep in a cool room. Your body will shut down and relax easier when the room temperature and more importantly your body temperature is not to extreme. For instance, taking a very hot bath immediately before bedtime will spike your body core temperature and stimulate central nervous system function, thus heightening awareness levels at a time when you should be trying to lower stimulation. So, it's not a good idea to take a hot bath before bedtime.

3. Mind your food and drink intake. Be smart about your food and drink consumption around bedtime. If you overeat or overdrink close to bedtime; your body will want to continue to digest, process, and eliminate during the night. This may leave you needing bathroom breaks during the night and with extra unwanted energy from any late-night snacks.

   Also avoid nicotine, caffeine, and alcohol where possible as they are all stimulants and will dehydrate you.

4. Wind down. Turn off high drama TV, stop surfing the Internet, and turn off all electronic devices about one hour before bedtime as part of your ritual. Research suggests that screen time or other media use before bedtime interferes with sleep.

5. Best way to fall asleep. If your mind is overrun with thoughts and you are finding it hard to relax, I would suggest that you focus on your breathing. Start by making the duration of your in-breath match the

duration of your out-breath. Give your brain the simple task of counting up to four on the in-breath and back down to one on your out-breath. Just keep this cycle of breathing going and then make your breath flow as smooth and even as possible. This should be enough to help you drift off to sleep in a very short space of time.

If I find myself struggling to sleep, I will read a book until my eyes start to feel tired, and then I start the breathing exercise above works every time for me.

3: GETTING THE BASICS RIGHT

Before you start out on any training plan, there are some "Important General Training Guidelines" that should be put in place immediately. For someone who is just about to embark on a running program these guidelines will form the backbone of how to train efficiently and safely. Below, I have compiled a quick reference list of some of the key points for you to follow when getting started.

TIME YOUR FOOD INTAKE CORRECTLY

I would recommend waiting for about two hours after a meal before running. Two hours is enough time for food to empty from the stomach, especially if it's high in carbohydrate. However, a protein food source will be a little easier and quicker to digest. If you don't wait long enough, food will not be properly digested, and you will run the risk of abdominal cramps. You will also miss out on the valuable energy that your last meal could have provided you before you go for your run.

STICK TO THE FOOD AND ROUTINES YOU KNOW

Don't eat or drink anything new before or during a race or hard work out. Only try new foods or make changes to your established routine when you can afford to go easy and there will be no serious repercussions. Always use the systems that work best for you.

WARM UP AND COOL DOWN CORRECTLY

Start every session with the exercises in the Warm Up section of this book and then move into 10 minutes of walking or slow running. You should always do the same for your cool down. A Warm Up system prepares your body for exercise by gradually increasing blood flow and raising core muscle temperature. The cool down part of your routine is every bit as important. It will help the muscles release the extra unneeded energy that you have just created, and if you stop abruptly, it can cause leg cramps and possibly nausea too.

RUNNING THE FIRST LEG INTO THE WIND

The key is to monitor your effort, not your pace on windy days. A headwind will always slow you down more than a tailwind will speed you up. But more importantly if you start your run with the wind behind your back you will generate a lot of heat and the moisture you produce can then lie on your skin. Once you turn to face into a cool breeze, there will be a rapid cooling effect. As result, your body will use more energy to keep you warm. The more energy you use, the more fuel you burn (food is fuel), which in turn can lead to what's known as a "hunger knock" (feeling hungry while exercising) and can lead to a feeling of lightheadedness and lack of energy.

If you set off with a tailwind, you are likely to run farther away from your base (home, the gym, the office etc.) and may find yourself going too far and having to battle beyond your capabilities to get back. What happens is that the tailwind pushes, you to run faster and you get a false sense of running fast and feeling good because of the km split times you are running. When you turn around to face the run back to base into the wind, you feel tired having run the first half of your session too fast.

SET AND KEEP AN EVEN PACE

The best way to race to a personal best is to maintain an even pace from start to finish. As you get more experienced you will learn how to finish with a "negative split" this just basically means that you will run the second half of your race deliberately faster than the first portion and therefore finish faster. So, once your warm up is complete, start the watch and keep a smooth and even pace. If you set out too fast, you will almost always pay for it later. Make sure to control the urge to run fast in the early stages of an endurance event. This can be difficult, especially if you have been building up and training hard for a sustained period for a specific event (i.e. marathon). Don't get caught up in the emotion and energy surge all around you that always results in a start line stampede.

OBSERVE THE CONVERSATION RULE

You should be able to talk in complete sentences while running. Studies have found that runners whose heart and breathing rates were within their target aerobic zones could comfortably carry out a conversation. Those who couldn't were running faster than optimal. Obviously, talking should not be easy during hard runs, speed work, or races.

IMPROVING RUNNING TIMES - CROSS TRAINING

Cross-training and weight training will make you a stronger and healthier runner. Runners who only run are prone to injury. Other low intensity sports like biking and swimming will help build supporting muscles used in running. Please pay attention to your core muscles while in the gym and make sure to use the set of Stability Exercises in this book daily or as often as you train. This sort of balanced approach to training will also give your primary running muscles time to rest and repair. However, if your time is limited, devote most of it to running.

TRAINING SHOULD REFLECT YOUR GOALS

The most effective training method to use is to mimic the event and distance for which you're training. This really is the golden rule of training for any activity. If you want to run a 5K at a set pace, you need to do some running at that exact pace.

MATCH YOUR GEAR TO THE WEATHER

The general dress code for a run is to dress as if it is 10 degrees warmer than the thermometer actually reads. Or, dress for how warm you'll feel at mid-run– not at the start of a run when your core temperature is still heating up. This means choosing the right apparel for the right weather conditions. On warm days, wear a lightweight performance fabric next to your skin, which will disperse sweat through evaporation and layer up with the right gear as temperatures change from season to season.

Here's a quick chart to help you dress appropriately for your runs, no matter what the weather. Please be sure to factor wind chill into your gear selection.	
TEMP	BASIC APPAREL
above 70	Lightweight singlet and shorts
60 to 69	Tank top or singlet and shorts
50 to 59	T-shirt and shorts
40 to 49	Long-sleeve shirt and shorts
30 to 39	Long-sleeve shirt and tights
20 to 29	Two upper-body layers and one lower-body layer

10 to 19	Two upper-body layers and one lower-body layer
0 to 9	Two to three upper-body layers, one/two lower-body layers
below 0	Time to go indoors for a cross-training gym session

INVEST IN THE RIGHT PAIR OF RUNNING SHOES

When you have the correct gear on, it will allow you to train properly. You also need to pay attention to your choice of footwear. The average lifespan of a pair of running shoes is about 400 km (250 miles), and the best advice I can offer on this topic is to go to your local sports shop and get professionally fitted. Make sure not to lace up your runners to tightly as your feet will swell slightly as they heat up during your run.

BUILD MILEAGE GRADUALLY

If you over-train you are more likely to get injured and give up before you have had time to see the positive benefits that running can have on your physical and mental well-being.

KEEP A TRAINING LOG

Always keep track of your training sessions. This is not just for the professionals. It will allow you to look at your progress and see what is working best for you. It will also provide a strong sense of motivation for you when you can look back on your starting point and see just how far you have come.

THE REFUELING RULE

Consume a combination carbohydrate-protein food or beverage within 30 to 60 minutes after any race, speed workout, or long run. Make sure to top-up on carbohydrates to replace depleted muscle glycogen. Glycogen forms an energy reserve that can be quickly mobilized to meet a sudden need for glucose. So, it is important to replace these carbs post-workout and add some protein to repair and build muscle. Ideally, the carb-protein ratio should be 4-parts carbohydrates to 1-part protein. Try a recovery sports drink, flavored yogurt, or a bagel and peanut butter to kick start your muscle repair.

My SportsMax supplement will greatly assist in speeding up your performance and recovery times. The full description of SportsMax is in the supplement section.

REST DAYS ARE TRAINING DAYS TOO

Rest days should be seen as part of your training system. It is imperative that you give your body enough time to repair the damaged muscle fibers before a training session. Otherwise you will not be in a position to get the maximum benefits from your next workout.

JOIN A RUNNING GROUP

This is worth repeating. "When you are just getting started or have not built a running regimen, it is a good idea to join a running group." The group will provide you with local knowledge and more importantly the motivation to keep going when things get tough, not to mention a good social network of like-minded people.

4: HEALTHY WORKOUT TIPS

1. Before you start your training session – use the Warm Up sequence of exercises. This will help you wake up all the small stabilizer muscles that support the larger muscle groups. Then, with all your muscles woken up and supported properly you will be better physically prepared to move into the more active stage of your warm up sequence. This "pre-warm up" sequence is often neglected and can lead to underperforming during training sessions and possible injuries.

2. If you are taking an indoor session, I would recommend that you start with the warm up, and then move into the main body of your work out. At this stage you can incorporate the stability series of exercises, which are designed to promote a strong core. A strong core is essential in helping runners maintain a strong posture and harness the strength of the shoulders/arms with that of the glutes and legs.

3. Once you have completed your indoor or outdoor session, you should have a very clear cool down routine organized. I would recommend decreasing the intensity of your session steadily until you are in a position to walk about 500m. Then use the 9 recovery exercises in this book to help take tension out of your lower back, hips, and legs. As you release the tension from these areas, you will improve the body's ability to circulate good and bad fluids. Being able to remove the buildup of lactic acid from muscles after training sessions

quickly and clearing the path for nutrition rich blood to flood and repair your muscles, ligaments, tendons, and joints will greatly improve your recovery time and get your body ready to perform at its optimum level for your next training session. Once you have completed your cool down exercises, you need to use the hot/cold shower (at least on your legs and lower back) and get the correct nutrition in.

4. You can also use the sequence of 27 exercises as a perfect, free flowing, stand-alone exercise workout program, safe in the knowledge that you will be stronger and better prepared for your next session- whatever your chosen sport.

WORKOUT SUPPORTS

- Eat Wheat germ to help rebuild muscle fiber.
- Put 1 x 30c Arnica remedy in your water bottle and drink during workout. This will improve stamina and help to heal bruising immediately.
- Take a good quality pre | post workout shake to help muscle recovery. This will remove soreness and allow you to train harder.
- Use your shower in a hot | cold sequence. 2 min hot / 1 min cold. This helps blood flow. Finish with cold water.
- Drink correct water amounts each day. Remember a slight thirst indicates a reduction of up to 20% of your efficient energy output and concentration.

To calculate your optimal daily water intake,

visit **www.QuantumFlowPerformance.com/runningbook**

to download your free guide to better hydration.

Start your recovery plan as soon as you have finished your last routine.

- Keep acid levels in your body to a minimum. This will decrease joint inflammation and improve mobility
- Drink Nettle Tea instead of tea | coffee during the day.
- Here are some useful Homeopathic remedies I like to use
- For Head Injuries take Arnica 30c
- For Lower Back Pain take Rhus Tox 30c. 1 before rest as required.
- For Tendon/Ligament Injuries take Arnica immediately followed by Hypericum for pain and Ruta to heal ligaments.

YOUR HOMEWORK

Establish a post-workout routine and see it as part of your new training system. It is every bit as important as any exercise you will have just done in training. Prepare your post-workout snack before you start the workout. That way you are sure to take it and improve your healing process.

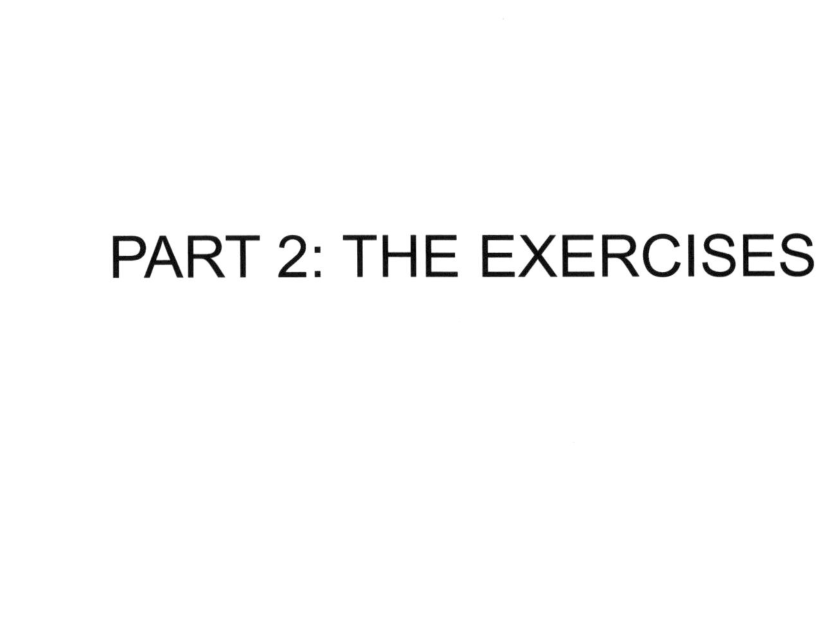

PART 2: THE EXERCISES

5: CORRECT RUNNING TECHNIQUE

Achieving the correct running technique is the most important part of maintaining injury free running. As soon as your body starts to fatigue, you lose your perfect form. The key to being able to achieve and sustain a good running technique hinges around cultivating strength and flexibility in equal measures. This provides you with balance in your overall body and elasticity in every muscle. This balance starts and ends with correct posture. Strong core muscles act like an elastic band gently wrapping and supporting your torso from the inside out.

The first thing I do is help my clients find out what "Neutral Spine" feels like. This is where the spine is aligned in the correct position to support the length of the spine and weight of the head (503). It is neither too far forward (501) nor too far back (502).

fig 501 fig 502 fig 503

Now that you have achieved a neutral spine, you must align it with your upper spine. To do this, we place one hand (palm up) on your belt line and place the other hand (palm down) across your sternum (breast bone). Keep the lower hand still and adjust your upper body to locate the hands directly above each other.

The next step is to place your elbows down by your sides and allow your elbow joints to open to approximately 100 degrees. By keeping your elbows close to your side and moving them in a relaxed straight line, you will improve forward momentum and stability while you run. Keep your shoulders relaxed and your hands soft.

It's very important to maintain a slight forward lean (about 5 degrees at the top of your head). This lean comes from your heels up and not just from the waist up. So, when you start to practice this technique for the first time, make sure to practice over short distances first and then build up to a complete run. This will allow you to use gravity to promote forward motion instead of your legs doing all the work. Your legs now only have to support you as you move forward.

FOOT PLACEMENT

Correct foot placement is very important and should be learned first and then practiced mindfully with every step.

It is best to avoid over-striding as this could lead to your heel landing first on the ground. That is when you connect with the ground heel first. The result is your heel acts like a brake. You slow down, and your joints absorb a greater impact than necessary.

Focus on lifting your heel up behind. For shorter distances and greater speed, you will then need to lift your knee forward and upward. Aim to place your foot to land directly in a straight line from your head through your core, hip, and knee joint. The higher the heel lift the less surface contact you generate and the faster you go.

Now you need to make sure that your shoulders are

relaxed and placed down away from your ears. This will help to take the tension out of your upper body and lead to better lung capacity and more oxygen. Have your arms and hands remain soft and relaxed with a 100-degree angle on the inside of your elbow. Your elbows should then swing in a controlled forward manner between chest and waistline.

BREATHING EXERCISE

Many people forget to focus on their breathing. Deep belly breathing is the best way to improve lung capacity quickly and should be part of every training system. Your body demands more oxygen when you exercise; so, how much oxygen you can deliver to your muscles will ultimately decide how well you can run. On top of that, as your muscles work hard while running, they produce toxic waste. Your exhale is a great way to get rid of some of the negative build-up.

Focus on your Breath.
After all, you can live for fifty days
without food, five days without water,
but only five minutes without oxygen.

I recommend practicing simple breathing techniques once a day so that while we are getting ready on the outside, we are also getting ready on the inside. Start by inhaling for a ten second breath and holding it at the top for ten seconds, and then slowly exhale for ten seconds. If you find this too difficult reduce the second counts but keep them equal, so in for 4, hold for 4 and out for 4. Slowly start to build up and you will soon notice a difference.

The great thing about this exercise is that it can be done anywhere. If I am waiting somewhere and find myself with time on my hands, I do this breathing exercise. Not only do I feel energized afterwards, but I also feel that I have just got a little extra workout in. Yoga gurus have taught for ages that a one hour focused breathing session can deliver an extra ten days of vitality over a lifetime. Imagine doing this once a week!

Finally, please make sure to warm up well before beginning any training routine. The correct warm up is critical to helping improve your running technique. It takes time to elevate your heart rate safely from sitting to running. As your heart rate rises, you start to push more fuel (blood) around your body. Simple active stretching exercises will loosen up joints and help to free up tension from your muscles and connective tissue. This will allow for greater mobility and bring you closer to the optimum running technique.

To achieve an economical running style, imagine a line between your legs, running down from your groin area to the floor. Each foot needs to land either side of that line for optimal performance.

6: CORE CONTROL

Very simply put, Quantum Flow Running is the art of mindful training. After many years of teaching Pilates to age groups ranging from 8 to 60 + years old, I realized that the most efficient way to train is to bring your mind into every move before you even start to physically perform the move.

Firstly, that involves being clear as to exactly what muscle groups you are going to be working. The exercises target specific muscle groups.

Secondly, you need to slow down the movement to avoid losing control of your form.

Thirdly, you need to work on completing each repetition with the highest amount of accuracy possible. This is important because it will create a baseline from which you can track progress in your performance. When you practice using the correct form for an exercise or movement continuously the correct movement becomes ingrained into your fibers. Then if you happen to do something wrong as a result of being pulled out of alignment due to momentum you have a correct baseline to measure from.

The perfect place to start practicing and perfecting this technique is with activating your core. Your core muscles are the deep muscles in your lower torso that support multi-dimensional movement.

This type of natural internal support system is vital for correct movement and provides maximum strength while exercising. Having studied and taught Pilates for many years, I have found that this style of movement can greatly improve core strength and overall body flexibility. Pilates is all about staying true to the correct techniques and not over doing each exercise.

HOW TO ENGAGE YOUR CORE

The sequence for getting your core engaged is a simple six step process, and it is vital that you keep it engaged for the duration of each exercise when indicated.

Step 1: Take a full belly breath; in through your nose and fill up your tummy region.

Step 2: Start to exhale and as the air leaves through your mouth draw your navel back towards your spine and upwards.

Step 3: Focus on a point 2 inches below your navel and make sure the muscles there feel strong and engaged.

Step 4: Now breathe high into your back to keep air out of your core area. This will allow you to keep your core muscles active for the duration of the moves.

Step 5: Take another high breath into your back as you prepare to move.

Step 6: Exhale as you move.

If you would like to get a visual demonstration of this and other techniques, then please go to my website at:

www.Quantumflowperformance.com/runningbook

for videos and other resources on this topic.

The duration of your breath always matches the duration of your move

---

7: WARM-UP SYSTEM

Your warm up routine is what will set the tone for your workout. When you send the right signals to your muscles during the warm up phase, you communicate an important message to the level of impending performance you expect in the next couple of minutes and hours from your body. It is a call to action, if you will.

The warm up routine is designed to activate the small muscle groups that stabilize your body and also over a longer period will greatly improve efficiency of function. With just 9 simple exercises that take less than 10 minutes in total, you will wake up your body and prepare it for action.

Perform these exercises each time you run.

1. SPINAL BEND

Builds flexibility through the spine.

Starting position: Stand tall with your hands stretched over your head (fig 701).

Movement: Reach towards the sky and then start to fold from the waist. Continue to reach forward and out and then out and down. (fig 702). Take 3 deep breaths. Tuck chin to chest and peel gently up through the spine taking care to stack your vertebra one at a time.

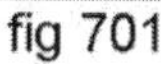

fig 701

fig 702

2. VERTICAL ARM RAISE

Builds flexibility in the shoulder and stretches the upper back and arms.

Starting position: Stand tall with your hands together in the praying position (fig 703). Make sure that your hands, forearms, and elbows are joined together.

fig 703

Movement: Raise your hands upward while keeping your elbows together for as long as possible. As soon as your elbows start to vibrate allow them to separate slowly, but still keep them as close as possible as they move overhead. Stretch high and inhale deeply at the top (fig 704).

fig 704

Now bring arms down while trying to get elbows and forearms back together as soon as possible (fig 705).

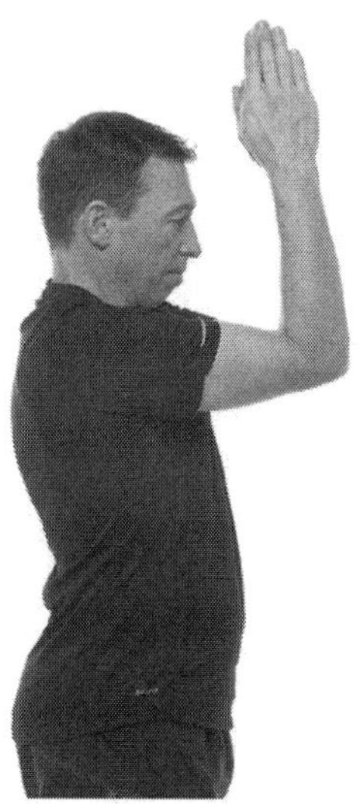

fig 705

Tip: Don't force the movement. Keep it fluid. Only allow a small amount of vibration into your shoulders.

3. SIDE KNEE DROP

Builds mobility and strength in torso by disassociating hip and shoulder movement.

Starting position: Lie on your back with arms and shoulders flat on the mat, bend your legs at the knees, and extend arms out at your sides (fig 706).

fig 706

Movement: Lower your bent legs to the right until they touch the floor (fig 707 - fig 708), pause for three counts, raise to the center, and then lower to the left.

fig 707

fig 708

Repeat six reps on each side.

Tip: Abdominals contracted and shoulders back. Always breathe out when you move.

*** If you suffer from lower back issues please keep feet in contact with the floor or mat at all times***

4. I.T. BAND STRETCH

To improve flexibility in the hips, glutes, and IT bands (the muscle band that runs from thigh down to outside of knee and attaches to tibia. IT means "iliotibial").

Starting position: Lie on your back with your knees bent and your feet flat on the floor.

Movement: Cross and rest left ankle onto and slightly over right knee (fig 709). Now place left hand between legs and right hand around outside of right leg. Join hands if possible and draw right leg towards you while using left elbow to push the left knee in opposite direction.

fig 709

fig 710

Hold position for 5 seconds and repeat 3 times then swap sides (fig 710).

Tip: Stay high on your shoulder blades and keep your shoulders square. Exhale as you stretch.

5. LYING HAMSTRING STRETCH (CORE ENGAGED)

To warm up your hamstrings, quads, and engage all stabilizing muscles into the glutes. Brings increased blood flow into lower back and surrounding lower core muscles.

Starting position: Start on your back with your legs outstretched and your hands by your sides.

Movement: Draw knees into table top position and then extend legs into a vertical position (fig 711). You should exhale and ease forward onto your shoulder blades while placing both hands onto one leg.

fig 711

Lower one straight leg to within 3 centimeters of the floor and use both hands to draw vertical leg in an overhead direction (fig 712).

fig 712

Tip: Make sure to exhale when lengthening the hamstring and inhale when lowering the leg. Keep a steady rhythm and maintain control.

Caution: This move can put pressure on a previously weakened back so don't lower legs as much if working with a lower back injury or condition.

6. LATERAL HEEL FLICK

To lengthen and strengthen core muscles, to stretch chest, quads, hips, and abdominals and to activate the Gluteus Maximus.

Starting position: Lie face down with your arms spread out (fig 713).

fig 713

Movement: Thrust your left heel towards your right hand keeping your right hip glued to the floor (fig 714).

fig 714

Tip: Squeeze glutes as you thrust left heel towards right hand.

7. EXTENDED PRESS-UP WALK

Builds shoulder and core stability. Also lengthens hamstrings, calves, and lower back muscles.

Starting position: Stand with legs straight and hands on floor. (fig 715)

fig 715

Movement: Keeping your legs as straight as possible and abdominals contracted. Walk your hands out. Keeping your legs straight, walk your feet back up to your hands (fig 716, fig 717 and fig 718).

fig 716

fig 717

fig 718

Tip: Use short steps on the walk back up to your hands.

8. EXTENDED FORWARD LUNGE AND STRETCH

Improve flexibility in your hips, hamstrings, lower back, torso, groin, hip flexors and quadriceps.

Starting position: Take large step forward with right leg (lunge), place and support your weight with your left hand in line with your right foot (fig 719).

fig 719

Movement: Take your right elbow and reach down to your instep of forward right leg keeping your back knee off the floor. Move your right hand to the instep of your right foot and twist your left arm in an extended position until it is fully extended upwards (fig 720). Now place both hands on the floor and bring your left foot forward. Come back to a standing point. Then step forward into your next lunge and repeat on alternate sides for a total of ten reps.

fig 720

Tip: Keep your back knee off the floor and make sure both hands are in contact with floor as you start to lift your hand off the floor for second part of the movement which stretches your hamstrings and calves.

9. DROP LUNGE

Use this drill to open up the muscles in your hips and groin area.

Starting position: Stand balanced with arms extended out in front of you and engage your core.

Movement: From a standing position, take a large step out to the right. Make sure to keep your feet flat and your chin up with a flat back. Keep your left leg straight and shift your weight onto your right leg (fig 721). Bend right leg at the knee to activate the stretch. Switch legs and repeat.

fig 721

Tip: Hold on each side for 3 seconds and repeat 6 times on each side.

In our next chapter I will share with you a set of exercises that will build stability, improve flexibility, and greatly boost your overall performance. A great way of staying motivated is to track the improvement in your degree of flexibility.

The best way to warm up your feet is to do two sets of stabilized heel lifts, followed by a twenty second ankle wobble exercise on both feet. A description of them follows in the stability exercises section.

Don't be tempted to take short cuts.

As with any new routine, it will take a little time to come to grips both mentally and physically with the sequence and techniques of this format. However, the benefits of starting a session in this controlled way will give you an opportunity to get into the main part of your session safely and aware of muscle groups that may still not have fully recovered from your last session.

Reduce the risk of groin strain by 10% for every 1 degree gained in your hips range of motion.

8: STABILITY EXERCISES

Once your muscles start to get more flexible and move more freely, you will need to focus on bringing stability into your core muscles in order to correctly support every movement you make. Bear in mind that our organs and all the internal workings of our body move when we move, exercise, and even breathe. On a normal breath, our lungs expand. In order to facilitate this movement and make space for the air intake, our liver should move 3 to 5cm on a deep breath. All of our internal organs need the flexibility to move freely in order for us to perform to the best of our ability. By just using these simple exercises below you can simply improve not just your health but also your workout or competitive performance.

Perfect practice makes perfect form.

---

1. KNEELING CORE EXERCISE

This exercise will help you to understand the principle of true core engagement and will also tone the lower transverse or belt line core muscles.

Starting position: Kneel down onto all fours. Make sure that you have a nice flat back and keep your neck straight as you look to the floor. The great thing about starting with this exercise is that there is no movement... no distractions.

fig 801

Movement: Fill your tummy with air and as you exhale make sure you engage the belt line area by lifting the navel up and back towards the spine (fig 801). With no air in the body and a very tight core area, hold your empty breath for 10 seconds. Take a breath in and activate the core on the next breath.

10 repetitions

Tip: Stay still and focus on getting maximum tension into your core.

2. HUNDREDS

This is a primary movement from the Pilates model, and it is designed to warm up the body while increasing abdominal strength. It will also bring stability into your torso and lower back.

Starting position: Lie on your back with your hands down by your sides, knees bent, and feet flat on the floor. Now WITH YOUR CORE ENGAGED raise your arms to about 3 inches off the floor and then as you breathe out, raise your head and neck up off the floor.

fig 802

You must also make sure your lower back is flat on the mat. Raise your legs into a tabletop position (fig 802). Make sure to keep core (stomach muscles) active throughout.

Movement: Drive your shoulders down towards your hips in order to keep high on your shoulder blades. Slowly move your strong rigid arms a short distance up and down to create tension in the lower core (belt line area). Take 5 short sniffing breaths in through your nose and then 5 short sharp exhales through your mouth. Each set is made up of 10 breaths. 10 sets of 10 breaths will give you the grand total of 100 breaths.

Tip: Keep lengthening through your fingers. Tummy stays strong. Engage your mind throughout the exercise.

3. THE ROLL UP

To improve total spinal flexibility and increase core strength.

Starting position: Lie on your back with your arms long overhead and legs flat on the mat. Make sure your lowest rib is in contact with the mat (fig 803).

fig 803

You might need support of a towel under the lower spine to help you do this move.

fig 804

Movement: Start to breathe in and raise your hands towards the ceiling as you move up onto your shoulder blades. Tuck chin to chest and squeeze your thighs together. Now start to lower hands and breathe out as you continue to peel your spine off the mat (fig 804).

fig 805

Pause at the end of the stretch for a small breath (fig 805) and then exhale as you retrace your movement back down to the mat.

Tip: Make sure to push through your heels and drive your shoulders towards your hips on the way up and tuck your tailbone under on the way back down.

4. PERFECT ABDOMINAL CRUNCH

Increase core strength.

Starting position: Lie on your back with your hands gently resting behind your head. Raise your knees into a tabletop position. (fig 806). Fully engage your core muscles across the beltline.

fig 806

Movement: Start to drive your shoulders down towards your hips and move upwards onto your shoulder blades. Pause briefly at the top of the move (fig 807) and then slowly release back down about 20% of the way with a short breath inward to match the duration of the movement.

fig 807

Tip: Make sure there is no air trapped in the tummy space or you will not be able to get maximum benefit from this move.

Start with 2 x sets of 10 reps with a 30 second break between.

5. OBLIQUE CRUNCH

To improve strength in the oblique core muscles. Will allow greater shoulder control and stability in uphill and speed situations.

Starting position: Lie on your back with your hands gently resting behind your head, elbows facing outward. Raise your knees into a tabletop position. Fully engage your core muscles across the belt line (fig 808).

fig 808

Movement: Start to breathe out as you move into a forward, lateral arc. Aim to bring your armpit to your opposite knee (fig 809). This movement must have two movements to it; forward and across.

fig 809

Tip: Keep your hips stuck to the floor (no movement). Visualize lifting your oblique muscles across your body midline and drop your knees slightly to the opposite direction of the crunch for a little extra burn.

Start with 2 x sets of 10 reps with 30 seconds break between.

6. THE SAW

To strengthen your mid and upper back. Improve pelvic stability.

Starting position: Sit up tall with your legs straight in front and shoulder width apart. Make sure your core is activated and your lower back is well supported. Arms are positioned out to the side and are level to sternum (fig 810).

fig 810

Movement: Breathe out as you rotate your arms and trunk to the side. Continue to exhale as you reach forward, little finger to opposite little toe. Breathe in as you return to start position. Keep arms up in a straight line (fig 811).

fig 811

Tip: Maintain core connection and look behind you as you reach forward. Don't slouch.

1 x set of 12 reps

7. SIDE LEG LIFT

To strengthen the glutes, hip abductors, and lateral torso.

Starting position: Lie on your side in a straight line with your shoulders stacked and hips stacked. Use your top hand for support but be very light on it (the more pressure you put on to the floor the less work your core has to do) (fig 812).

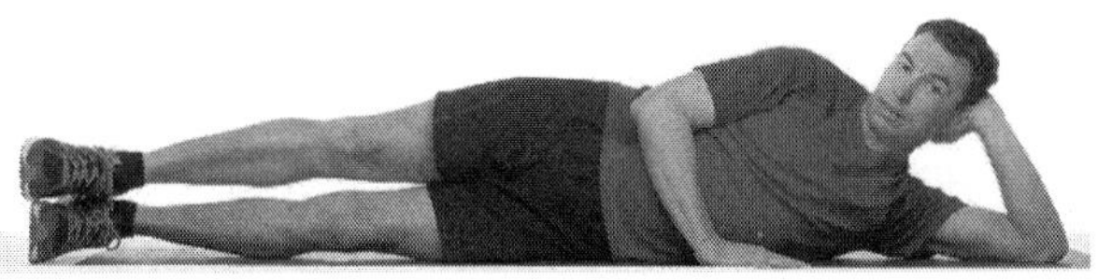

fig 812

Movement: Inhale as you prepare for the movement. Then exhale and raise both legs straight to maximum length (fig 813). Inhale as you bring leg back down to start position.

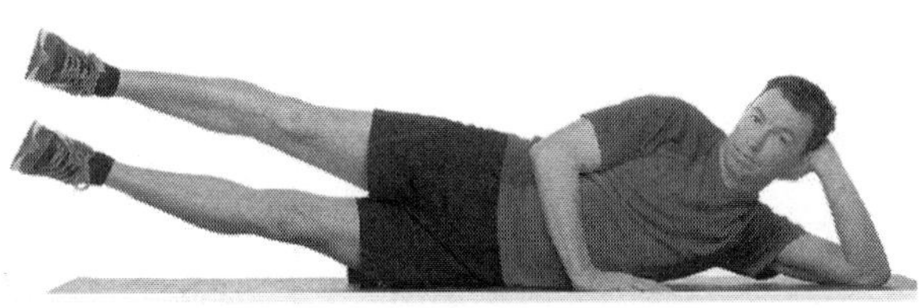

fig 813

Tip: Stay solid in the core and keep a straight line on the mat as you lift to the max with control.

Repeat for 10 times on each side, building up to 2 sets.

8. FORWARD BENT LEG STRETCH

To develop good core control and improve pelvic stability.

Starting position: Lie on your back with your knees bent and your feet flat on the mat.

Movement: Engage your core and bring both legs into the table top position (fig 814). Exhale and extend right in front of you while drawing left leg into a tuck position (fig 815).

fig 814

Now inhale as you swap leg positions, and at the end of the move draw the right into the body and exhale.

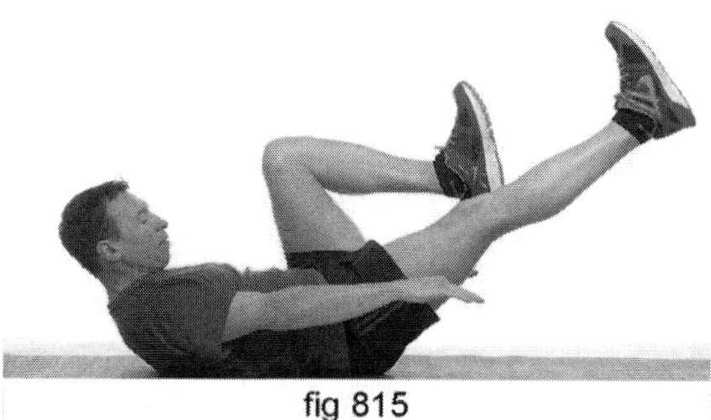

fig 815

Tip: Make sure that you keep your hips stable and control your leg movements from your core muscles.

Repeat 10 times.

9. ANKLE WOBBLE

To strengthen ankle ligaments and tendons.

Starting position: Standing upright with your core engaged.

Movement: Lift one foot off the ground and wrap it around the standing leg just below the calf (fig 816). If you are stable, then close your eyes and counter balance.

fig 816

Tip: Make sure core is correctly engaged and the area around you is safe in case you fall.

Do 2 x 20 second repetitions on each leg.

9: RECOVERY SYSTEM

Rest and recovery are very important parts of every training system. Our muscle fibers get torn as we exercise, and it is how we repair our muscle fibers during our downtime that dictates how well we will perform in our next session or match. Before we get into our exercise routines, it is important to understand the internal workings of our body and why we need to follow some other simple steps which will contribute greatly to our performance.

How to Achieve Your Training "Sweet Spot"

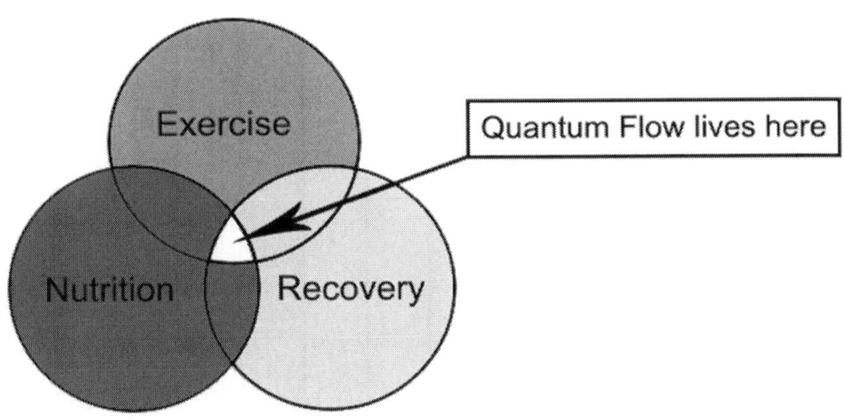

TRAIN | REPAIR | PERFORM

The key to achieving optimum sustainable health and performance lies in getting the balance of effort just right. The diagram above is broken down into 3 key components. Where these three circles intersect is the "Success Sweet Spot."

Preparing for an event is critical and can take a long time. Many hours are spent building a body that will perform to the best of its ability and match our expectations on a given day. We are all looking for a personal best come race day. But it is important to make sure that we reach the starting line not over-trained, tired, and sore. We must be fresh, enthusiastic, and full of energy. In order to give ourselves the best possible chance of reaching the start line in peak mental and physical shape we need to get these 3 keys components just right.

EXERCISE

We always focus on our correct Warm Up routine before every session. Our mission is to build elasticity into our muscle groups. This is done through flexibility and stability. It is; therefore, very important that this attention to detail is carried forward to our recovery exercise system as well.

NUTRITION

Nutrition plays a massive part in the body's recovery process. Recovery times can be sped up with the correct nutrition plan, thus allowing you to make bigger gains with every training session. Certain supplements can be of great value in this area. Most people lead a frantic lifestyle and find it hard to get the correct intake of daily nutrition from their meals alone. This is where the Quantum Flow range of supplements can help keep your body full of pure vitality inside and out.

For more information go to:
www.QuantumFlowPerformance.com

The recovery program that we follow in this book is designed to repair and nourish all your body's systems including the way your organs function. One of the body's key recovery tools is sleep. There has been much written and large amounts of research carried out on the value of sleep and the various stages of sleep cycles that our bodies flow in and out of every night. They have pinpointed which cycles are the most conducive to repairing and healing us, but for me there are really only a few things that you need to know about the art of getting a good night's sleep.

This is where we can save ourselves a lot of time and just take what the experts have found and apply it to our own lives:

Step 1: Switch off all Internet at least 90 minutes before bedtime.

Step 2: Reading a relaxing book (not a thriller) will help relax your mind.

Step 3: Practice a relaxation technique.

Step 4: Get an average of 7 to 8 hours sleep per night.

The following recovery exercises will continue to build flexibility and greatly speed up your recovery time, so you will be able to give every event your very best physical effort.

1. FORWARD SPINE STRETCH

To remove tension from spine. Release lower back tension and improve hamstring/calf muscle recovery by improving blood flow.

Starting position: Start in a seated position with your legs and arms straight out in front. (fig 901)

fig 901

Movement: Inhale and then as you start to stretch your hands forward slowly exhale. Make sure to keep your head up and only at the last second lower your head between your arms (fig 902). Inhale on the way back to the starting position.

fig 902

Tip: Make sure to lower your shoulders and squeeze your shoulder blades at the end of each rotation to maintain correct posture.

Repeat 10 times

2. BOW AND ARROW

To improve lung capacity and shoulder flexibility while gaining core control.

Starting position: Start in a seated position with your legs and arms straight out in front. (fig 903)

fig 903

Movement: Inhale to prepare for the move. Now exhale and draw your elbow towards and beyond your shoulder (fig 904).

fig 904

On the next inhale rotate torso and extend arm to full length behind you (fig 905).

fig 905

Then, return a straight arm back to the starting position.

Tip: Always look at your arm as it goes behind you and make sure you have a full lung at the end of every rotation.

Repeat 10 reps on each side. Working alternate sides.

3. THREE-WAY HAMSTRING STRETCH

3A. HAMSTRING STRETCH

To stretch the Hamstring, IT (Iliotibial) band, Upper legs + Glutes

Starting Position: Lie on your back with your head and both shoulders resting on the ground. Loop the rope around the ball of the foot and draw your leg to a relaxed vertical position.

Movement: As you breathe out, draw the rope, in a straight line overhead until your hamstring is fully extended. Hold this position for 3 seconds and inhale as you release the leg back just 4 inches or enough to release the immediate pressure from your hamstring muscle.

fig 906

Tip: Toes of both feet pointed towards the ceiling, one hand on the rope, the other hand flat on the ground.

3B. ADDUCTOR STRETCH

Starting Position: Lie on your back on the mat with a rope around your foot, wrapped around the inside of your ankle and looped under your leg.

Movement: Hold the rope with the hand on the same side as your working leg. Contract your glutes while you sweep your leg away from your body while inhaling. At the point of resistance give the rope a gentle pull. Exhale slowly while holding the stretch for 3 seconds.

fig 907

3c. GLUTE AND LOWER BACK STRETCH

The last in the series of three must do leg and hip stretches

Movement: Lie on your back on the mat with rope around your foot. Hold the rope with the hand on the same side as the leg you are stretching. Contract the inner thigh muscles of the working leg as you pull it across the body as far as you can. When you reach your full stretch pull on the rope to gently assist with a greater stretch. Exhale slowly while holding the stretch for 3 seconds and repeat at least 3 times.

fig 908

4. ROLL LIKE A BALL

To increase spinal flexibility, improve coordination and balance, and enhance pelvic stability.

Starting position: Start in a sitting up position with your knees bent and your feet off the floor. Keep the core activated and balance on your sitting bones (fig 909).

fig 909

Movement: As you exhale, pull the core muscles towards your spine and smoothly roll back as far as your shoulders (no higher) (fig 910). On the exhale start to roll forward to start position.

fig 910

Tip: Try to keep the move smooth and as you build flexibility into your spine, it will become easier to control.
As always practice makes perfect.

Repeat 10 reps – continuous.

5. SIDE LEG BIG CIRCLES

To increase flexibility and mobility in the hips and develop pelvic stability.

Starting position: Lie on your side in a straight line with your shoulders and hips stacked (fig 911). Use your top hand for support but be very light on it (the more pressure you put on the floor the less work your core has to do).

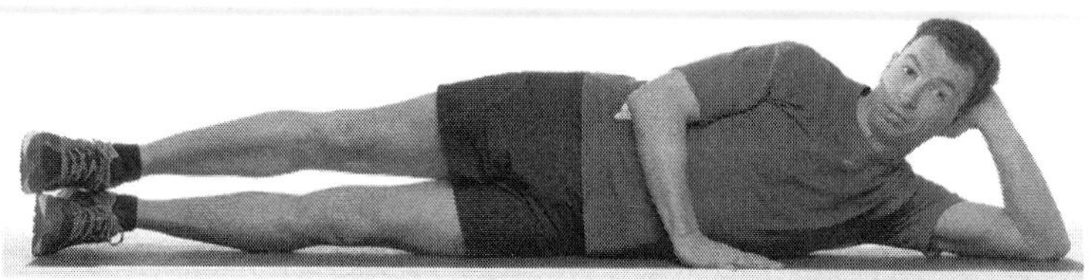

fig 911

Movement: Inhale to prepare for movement sequence. On the exhale raise the top leg to maximum lift (fig 912) and forward away from your body, then start to inhale and draw leg inward back to start (fig 913).

fig 912

fig 913

Tip: Go for maximum flexibility and keep core strong. Shoulders stay solid in stacked starting position.

Repeat 5 times and then change direction.

6. ALL 4S LIVER | SHOULDER STRETCH

To improve shoulder flexibility and lung capacity while stimulating internal organ function (i.e. liver and spleen).

Starting position: Kneeling on all fours, hands directly under your shoulders and knees under your hips, flat lower back (fig 914).

fig 914

Movement: Place left hand two inches behind right hand. Then as you exhale slide your left hand across body in the gap between right arm and leg (fig 915). On the inhale draw left hand back across body and lift a straight arm as high as possible (fig 916). Pause for two seconds.

fig 915

fig 916

Tip: It's important to keep a strong core and a straight lower back. No dip in lower spine. You should feel a big shoulder stretch on a full lung.

Repeat 8 times on both sides.

7. TWO-WAY SHOULDER STRETCH

To improve shoulder mobility and release tension from lung and chest area. Also improve liver mobility and clean blood flow.

Starting position: Lie on your side, with knees drawn up towards waist. Arms stacked in front, shoulder height away from your body (fig 917).

fig 917

Movement: Inhale as you draw one arm towards the ceiling (fig 918) and then exhale as your arm continues towards the floor in a sweeping motion. Rest at full extension for five seconds (fig 919). On next exhale lift arm back to start position.

fig 918

The second part of this exercise is activated from the same starting position (fig 917) and this time you sweep your hand up over your head (fig 920) and all the way around to the same end point (fig 919). Five second pause and return to start position as per move one.

fig 919

fig 920

Tip: Keep your knees glued to the floor. Always follow your hand with your line of sight.

Repeat 5 reps on each side.

8. TWO-WAY SPINAL STRETCH

To improve spinal mobility and encourage greater movement of spinal fluid to nourish the central nervous system.

Starting position: Kneeling on all fours. Straight spine and a flat lower back, hands under shoulders and knees under hips (fig 921).

fig 921

Movement: Inhale and look upwards as you allow your spine to sag towards the floor. Pause at the top for three seconds (fig 922).

fig 922

Exhale as you lower head and tuck chin to chest while arching your spine towards the ceiling (fig 923).

fig 923

Tip: Keep your core strong as this will activate the gallbladder and bile system, helping to clear toxins from your body quicker.

9. QUAD STRETCH

To stretch your Quad | Hip region. Improve circulation and release tension.

Start position: Lie on your stomach keeping non-working leg straight and resting on the floor.

Movement: Wrap the rope around the foot of your working leg. Grab the rope over your shoulder and pull leg upward. (fig 924). Contract your glute and hamstring muscles to stretch the quad and hip.

fig 924

Pull your heel towards the opposite glute (fig 925). Exhale slowly while holding the stretch for 2 seconds (fig 926).

fig 925

fig 926

Tip: Keep your knees close together to avoid putting unnecessary pressure on knee joint. Breathe correctly.

FOOT RECOVERY

The repair and relaxation of the feet are very important, and you should do these two simple exercises as they will greatly enhance recovery.

Place a tennis ball under your foot and gently roll the ball all over the sole. When you locate a sore point, stop there and apply pressure with the ball into that area.

Soak your feet in a basin of hot water with half a cup of Epsom salts dissolved in it, for ten minutes, once a week.

This foot soak is ideal after a long run or even after a long day at work.

PART 3: KEY PRINCIPLES

10: A DEEPER UNDERSTANDING

Holistic Running is all about taking into consideration every part of your body and improving its overall function. Your body can become tight and compressed due to several lifestyle factors; for example, stress, diet, and fatigue. Quantum Flow Running is all about becoming aware of what is going on in your body and being able to respond in a fast and accurate way to stay one step ahead of the physical, mental, and emotional problems. Most people fail to make the connection between emotional and physical fitness, but the reality is, it's very difficult to have one without the other. If you build up stress in your body; it restricts the production, flow, and distribution of your hormones, which can lead to emotional swings. So, Quantum Flow Running is about harnessing the sum of all the parts to create a machine that can move strongly and smoothly through any exercise or sport and carry those sporting benefits into your daily life.

TAKING CARE OF FASCIA - THE MISSING FACTOR

The mainstream approach to running, exercise, and movement to date has been very two-dimensional. It focuses on muscle function and joint movement. However, it is the fascia, or connective tissue in your body that gives you the ability to move in all directions. The fascia provides the 3-dimensional stability that you so greatly depend on for smooth, efficient movement. By removing restrictions from the fascia, you are in effectively removing the tension from your muscles and organs. That is why this 3D approach takes into consideration the optimal functioning of not just muscles and joints but also the fascia.

Your fascia holds all your organs in the correct place and allows them to move smoothly over each other. If you were to imagine one long single piece of lubricated "under skin" suit that wraps around every muscle and organ in your body, then you would have a good idea of what the fascia is like. This thin film of tissue is interconnected to every part of your body, from your skin to all your organs and muscles. Think of it as a tablecloth right under your skin. A pull on one corner of the tablecloth affects the shape and stability of the entire tablecloth.

To best illustrate how the fascia works, you need to be aware that whenever you take a breath, your lungs expand. To accommodate this expansion, your liver moves about 3 centimeters from its normal placement based on an average of 25k breaths per day. That's about 700 meters of movement per day! The smooth movement of your liver from point A to point B and back again depends on the correct functioning of the fascia. Even though the fascia is extremely strong, it is also prone to being pulled out of shape through tension. This can be exerted from any area of the body and can, in turn, exert tension on the spine and cause nerve supply to be impeded. Similarly, a tight calf muscle can induce a pull in the fascia that can radiate upward into your hip, leading to hip and lower back problems over time if not corrected. Ignoring this most important internal component can cause widespread dysfunction that will lead to injury and a lack of optimum mobility.

Let's look at a couple of the exercises from the program and see how they address taking care of your fascia.

Exercise 3 in the "Warm up" section "Side knee drop" seeks to isolate shoulder movement and improve your hip movement and mobility. There is a large band of deep strong fascia which diagonally connects the shoulder across to the opposite hip. When you perform this exercise regularly, you are removing any tension that may have built up from running, driving, or even sitting at a desk all day. Even though you are not actually directly stretching an obvious muscle, you are stretching out and warming up the fascia that is vital for smooth hip movement and that will definitely reduce the risk of injury.

Also, if we look at exercise 6 in the "Stability" section "The Saw," you will see how the move works certain muscle groups like those in the mid/upper back and pelvic region to improve lower back and hip stability. What you would not be aware of is that as you rotate your neck to look backwards towards the end of the move, you are releasing tension from the pocket of fascia that surrounds the thymus gland. The thymus is a key player in keeping a strong and healthy immune system. If the fascia becomes tight around the thymus, it can lessen its effectiveness.

There are many layers and multiple benefits to doing each exercise- some work big visible muscle groups and others work on small but massively important organs and glands. But, rest assure that each exercise has been carefully chosen to deliver optimum gains. With every organ, muscle, and gland having fascia wrapped around them you can see how important it is to take the fascia into consideration.

Training deep core muscles will teach your body to react faster and stronger in nearly every aspect of sport, especially in movements that require speed and agility like acceleration and sprinting.

11: PRINCIPLES OF MOVEMENT

Gravity is the key to movement and being able to use it to your benefit will improve your running ability. It is all around us. It affects everyone and everything. When running, it can work for or against us. So, let's make it work for us.

If you can introduce a tiny lean forward from your ankles while you run your body goes slightly off balance and starts to fall forward. This slight lean forward allows us to take advantage of gravity. Then instead of us using our legs to lift our full body weight every step of the way, we can reduce the length of our stride and speed up its cadence. This allows us to harness and use gravity to pull us forward faster with less effort, and we can use our legs to balance and support our body weight. This technique preserves lots of energy and allows us to run farther and faster with no extra effort.

Gravity also pulls a lot of toxins down towards the feet which makes this area even more susceptible to malfunction, not just in the feet, but transferring up through the whole body. When we train and repair the muscles in our feet, we provide a stable strong foundation to move freely on. Any misalignment of the feet can be transferred upward through the legs and into the lower back. This can greatly reduce full body flexibility, making your fitness routine or sports training less productive. Good alignment of the feet is usually a combination of correct hip alignment and muscle groups that are equally developed to maintain the symmetry of movement and protect joints at the same time. The more flexible we are, the more elastic our muscles can become, and the more efficient our performance can also become.

I have placed a lot of emphasis on core connection in this book and with good reason. Through a strong core connection, you can amplify the volume of strength that individual muscle groups can generate and also connect them to other muscle groups, thus building a much stronger platform from which to exercise from. Think of it as strengthening a web of interconnected fiber and tissue, where the synergy created gives you exponential power, flexibility, and endurance.

The most important physical and tangible part of moving correctly is that your posture is correct, making sure your spine, your hip, and your extremities are all properly aligned. Also, that your feet are in the best possible condition. This fact is widely ignored, but if you think of the amount of pressure that we put our feet under every day standing, walking, and not just while running, you will see how important it is to train and repair your feet on a regular basis.

The Warm Up exercises listed in part 2 are just one of three very important principles of movement in my 3D training system. These exercises can have massive benefits on your performance ability.

The small stabilizer muscle groups in your body are often neglected because of incorrect training techniques and due to a disproportionate focus on the large muscle groups, which makes us look good. This is particularly true of the small stabilizer muscles located in the thoracic area of the back. Because most people tend to suffer from either upper or lower back problems, I tend to focus on these areas during rehabilitation. However, most of the problems, in my opinion, come from the mid back and its inflexibility. With restricted movement in the mid back, we tend to rely on our large muscle groups for regular movement. Yet these large and strong muscles provide us with a lesser degree of flexibility and mobility because they are designed to support and move large areas of bones.

You need to learn how to recruit these small stabilizer muscles and encourage them to do their job so you can voluntarily switch off the large muscle groups that are overcompensating for their smaller sized cousins. When you fire them up, they provide extra support and much greater strength for your large muscles to reach their maximum power potential.

The exercises in this book are designed to bring a greater degree of flexibility into your bodies while increasing blood flow to all muscle groups which are needed during intense active movement. Together with the correct breathing technique and the correct activation of your large muscle groups, they promote stability to your musculoskeletal system.

The optimum cadence or number of foot strikes per minute when running is 182. What is yours?

12: GETTING MOTIVATED

"Man cannot discover new oceans unless he has courage to lose sight of the shore."

Andre Gide

This chapter contains the most important information for those of you who are just starting out on your running journey because without motivation there is no follow through. You have to be brave and look deep within in order to follow a new path.

A key part of being successful in this program is that you trust the information and techniques that I have provided long enough for you to lose sight of your old ways (the shore) and sail smoothly into a better place. I have found from previous experience that it takes about eight weeks to see sufficient rewards from a running program to create a sense of optimism and trust in your new routine/habit. So, this is what you will be aiming for.

The driving force behind the ability for you to create lasting change is motivation. Cultivating the correct sporting mindset and the correct attitude to running will test your resolve, but if you can master these motivation techniques and practice applying them successfully on a daily basis to help you overcome your exercise challenges, you will then be free to apply the exact same skills to other areas of your life that you may wish to change.

THE SCIENCE BEHIND CHANGING BEHAVIORS

Scientists have found that your brain finds it easier to build a new habit (neural pathway) rather than change an old one. You see, you become comfortable in your "comfort zone," and it can be difficult for people to leave that sense of comfort. The thing is that real growth happens when we leave that comfortable space, challenge ourselves and trust in our ability to survive, thrive, and succeed.

The reason for this type of behavior is very simple– your brain finds it impossible to voluntarily sever neural pathways (or connections) and finds it much easier to develop and build a new connection. Rather than trying to kill old habits you must grow new and more compelling ones by attaching positive emotions and positive self-talk to the new and successful habits that you want to form in your brain. Your ability to successfully develop these new neural connections is based on your brain's level of neuroplasticity.

Neuroplasticity is the ability of the brain to grow new neural pathways quickly and efficiently. If you want to learn a new skill, it is dependent on building a new neural pathway- the stronger the connection the better the skill. Better neuroplasticity means faster neural connections. Cells that fire together, wire together.

The biggest obstacle to forming a "new neural pathway" is stress (in my opinion). Stress compresses and restricts brain function. We need to release (decompress) stress patterns that have formed in the brain tissue- especially the "tentorium." We can overcome or release old negative stress patterns by revisiting old negative incidents that have happened to us and releasing or reconciling the negative trauma or event that may have stressed us out in the first place.

We can also use nutrition to help support brain function -we tend not to think of our brain needing nutrition, BUT it uses 20% of the body's total energy. We must always consider nutrition sources to support activity levels. Nutrition for the brain will also support the activation of new neural pathways.

Use supplements "Brain Power" and "All Day Energy" to support brain nutrition.

The way to create these new habits is to facilitate them by being clear on what actions need to take place, prepping so that everything you need to take action is there, and reinforcing your belief in your ability to achieve the success. You have a better chance of success if there is less disruption to the formation of a new neural pathway. The pathway makes sure the behavior works successfully and has a better chance of becoming part of daily life.

SCHEDULING AND MINDSET

The best exercise routines in the world cannot help you if they are not used. Without the sustained motivation to follow through in using these techniques on a regular basis, you will drift away. You will not give yourself a fighting chance to make lasting positive change to your overall health for years to come.

I need to make sure that you stay on top of your game at all times to avoid the sort of choices that will leave you feeling dejected and uninterested in your health and life. That is why we all must continue to forge new neural pathways and develop new positive skills and habits that replace the old negative ones.

You are all familiar with the saying "your health is your wealth." When you take some time to ponder the meaning of this phrase, you will start to realize just how important your health really is. So, to get you going on the right path to vitality in a time efficient manner, let's just set some short-term goals and let's stick to the mantra of taking things "one day at a time." This attitude will lead you to a greater chance of success than anything else out there.

Most people find the hardest part of a workout is the preparation. Just finding the time and getting ready to workout requires a lot of motivation and the fact that you have to look for your training gear and then change into cold, form-fitting clothing can put many people off. But once you are set and moving, your energy starts to flow, your mind and body become flooded with mood enhancing hormones, and you understand that it's always worth the effort because it makes you feel great about yourself and happy to be alive. You can store and use these positive feelings and a positive self-image which you have created and use at a later stage in the day or week if you need to get out of a negative space.

Here are some simple tips for organizing your agenda in advance so you can make exercise part of your weekly "must do" list.

Break down your agenda | scheduler | planner | calendar into 3 sections:

1. Meetings
2. Projects
3. Personal

In your "Personal" section of your agenda, schedule your exercise appointment (with yourself), the start time and duration of the session. My personal preference is to train in the morning because then I know that at least I have made progress in one of my goal areas on any given day. It provides me with an abundance of energy and motivation to tackle anything that the day has to offer me. This way you will start to give yourself the same respect as you do a work meeting. Through regular skilled practice you will see and feel the benefits of regular exercise in no time.

There are only two things that you should consider before heading out for a run. The first is: how are you feeling mentally and the second is: how are you feeling physically? If you can overcome the mental blocks and excuses that get in your way you will line yourself up for guaranteed success. You must continuously remind yourself that you "get to do this" you do not "have to do this." If you feel like you have to do something, be it, go for a run or clean your bedroom you will find a dozen reasons not to complete the task. However, if you tell yourself that you are getting this opportunity to keep yourself healthy and energized then you are likely to overcome any resistance that might have prevented you from achieving previous running and fitness goals in the past.

CLEARING RESISTANCE & BUILDING CONFIDENCE

The key to starting this process is that you must start to talk to yourself only in positive language. Words of encouragement that will move you towards your goals are the best way to stay on track. If you fill your head with words like "It's too cold" or "I'm too tired" or "It's not working" you will start to believe yourself, and as luck would have it- we act in accordance with our beliefs.

If we can stop our negative personal conversations and feed our self-talk with purely positive and successful language, we will be able to install a set of positive and successful beliefs which in turn will lead to a very strong mindset based on our training goals. Here's the best part – your performance levels will start to match your levels of belief. In other words, if you keep putting positive thoughts into your head you will start to believe them and then start to act in accordance with your beliefs. Shortly I will introduce you to the best way to plant positive self-talk in your mind

MANTRAS / AFFIRMATIONS

One of the fastest routes to raising your confidence and motivation is to use mantras or affirmations. It is not hard to see the effect of negative talk, people, and situations on our lives. The blues or even depression are very clear markers of the impact. Using positive affirmations is a proactive way of countering the results of negativity.

One thing you have absolute control over are your own thoughts. That's what puts you in a position to control your own destiny.

Affirmations are positive statements that we can repeat to ourselves in multiple ways on a daily basis. You can write them down. You can read them out loud. You can even listen to them. There are many affirmation audios out there. The important thing is to have the affirmation be relevant to what you are aspiring to achieve. If you are inclined to write your own personalized affirmations, I would recommend you follow these 6 simple guidelines.

AFFIRMATION GUIDELINES

- Start your affirmations with "I" or "My."
- Make your affirmations short so they're easier for you to remember.
- Write your affirmations in the present tense.
- Don't begin your affirmations with "I want" or "I need."
- Make sure all your affirmations are positive statements.
- Add emotional words to your affirmations.

Here are some of my favorite affirmations that I use on a daily basis for running. Maybe it would be a good idea to install one of the affirmations below or one of your own, on your screen saver, or as a welcome note on your phone to help you maintain focus on the task in hand:

- I enjoy my workouts and always feel better afterward.
- I feel better when I use the correct warm up exercises before each workout or competition.
- I always drink the right amount of water for my needs every day.
- I feel great when I start my recovery routine as soon as I finish every run.
- I always feel stronger when I include my stability exercises in my workouts.
- I love to eat healthy because it provides me with maximum energy.

For those of you have not used affirmations before, I recommend using them on a daily basis. You will notice the difference. I would ask you to place them at the top of your daily to-do list. In my opinion, they are the most powerful tool we have available to us. This allows us to build unwavering belief in our ability and greatly improve our performance levels in all we do.

FLEXIBLE MIND

We are all aware of the benefits of a flexible body at this stage of the book, and we now know what is required to achieve it. Now it's time to introduce you to some of the benefits of achieving a flexible mind and the steps required to achieve it:

Step 1: The ability to master the art of acceptance. When you accept a situation, it means that you have gained a clear, honest, accurate, and non-judgmental understanding of a situation. In other words, you have gained clarity.

Emotion clouds the mind and is usually propagated by Ego. For me, the letter E in ego stands for Emotion and the word Go implies movement or motion. So, Ego is Emotion in Motion.

When we remove emotion, we remove a large piece of ego and this allows us to gain a clear point of view. It allows us to honestly self-analyze and move forward, which is the whole point of the Quantum Flow Running Program. By getting a clear view of a situation, you can also get a clear and compelling view of what is wrong and what is right about the particular situation. It's important to focus on what is good first and then look at the negatives.

Step 2: Write down all the positive aspects first and then all the negative aspects that belong to the situation to see the state of play. This exercise will flag any reasons why you might need to change. And remember the more clarity we have the more power we have over the situation.

Step 3: Create an action plan. It is important to remain realistic. Think through any possible outcomes that may arise from actions you take and what those actions may have on others. Construct a step-by-step plan that will lead you to the desired resolution of the negative situation. You now have the power to move through every negative influence in your life and either change it to a positive one or maybe just remove it.

Step 4: Our life aspirations and needs are always evolving, so in order to accommodate these shifts and draw what we want to us, we must continually review our life path. This allows for maximum personal development. A good example of this would be to acknowledge the fact that the things that we thought were most important to us 5 years ago may no longer be of interest to us. For instance, last year's top fashion "must have" item that everyone wanted so badly (including you) is now forgotten and lying in the back of the wardrobe waiting to be discarded. In your 20s you would have laughed at the thought of having a financial advisor in your personal team, but maybe in your late 30s, you may seek one out as a must have in your arsenal of personal finance. Shifts happen throughout our lives for better or worse, so we need to learn to create positive experiences where possible and accept the things we do not have the power to change.

Now it's time for some action. After all, nothing is achieved without practice and implementation.

Write down a small situation that you would like to change:

Make a short positive and negative list in order to gain clarity and focus:

Now write the steps you need to take to change it:

Finally make sure that all changes and interactions will be carried out in such a way as to achieve mutual benefit. How are you going to do that?

____

____

____

____

____

____

____

____

____

When you have a little more time, you can sit down and take a bigger situation and go through the same process. But remember, the key for this system to work is to take action.

GOAL SETTING

So now that you have learned a system to change things that are already occurring in your life, it's time to learn a technique that will let you predict the future life you are going to grow into and that is goal setting. The reality is if you don't know where you are going you won't be able to find your way there. This applies to taking on running as much as any other aspiration.

Brainstorm what you really want in your life. It is important to focus on getting clear with your wants first before making any plans. When you edit yourself too soon, you will end up with a lackluster future that does not inspire you. This is a setup for failure. You will effectively block your progress by sending mixed signals to your brain and end up getting confused and giving up before you have even started the process of achieving your goals.

Time for another bit of action:

Write down 3 things that you would like to have in your life; one short-term, one medium-term and one long-term. Make sure they are precise and clear and not fueled by Ego. For example:

A Short-term Goal

- I am going to train for my running every Monday, Wednesday, and Saturday

Rather than just saying I will train three times per week– you need to nail it down to a schedule that is more specific and workable for you. If you just say that you will train three times per week you might be tempted to run very late in the week and then fail at the first hurdle.

A Medium-Term Goal

- I am going to eat healthy energy giving foods for the next three months.

At first glance you may feel that this goal is a stretch too far; however, if you take this goal back to one small step at a time, it becomes very doable. Just focus on the meal you are about to eat and make sure when before you go to the grocery shop that you write out a healthy shopping list. Only go shopping after you have eaten to avoid making impulse buys. If you don't buy the treats and don't bring them into the house in the first place, you will be less likely to cheat on your goal.

A Long-Term Goal

- I will complete my first 5k running race in 6 months' time.

If you look at the way these goals are stacked up, you will notice that there is a very good chance that you will achieve your long-term goal if you just look after your medium and short-term goals. So now it's your turn to set yourself some targets. Make sure to stack your goals and write them up in your daily and weekly planner to ensure they happen.

A - Short–term ______________________________

B - Medium–term ______________________________

C - Long–term ______________________________

Now, for each running/fitness goal, write down 3 actions that need to be taken for your short, medium, and long-term goals. Where you are in your fitness/well-being journey will define what steps, you need to take.

Short-Term Actions

A 1: ______________________________

A 2: ______________________________

A 3: ______________________________

Medium-Term Actions

B 1: ______________________________

B 2: ______________________________

B 3: ______________________________

Long-Term Actions

C 1: ______________________________

C 2: ______________________________

C 3: ______________________________

Once you have the list of actions you want to take, place a time frame on it, and if you are doing this journey with others, tell them.

Accountability is a great way of making sure that you stick to the desired process that will help you achieve your training goals. By telling a few very supportive people in your life about your goals you will be pushed to achieve the targets you have set yourself. Most people do not like letting people, especially family and close friends down, and that's exactly what it will feel like to you if you have publicly declared your intentions.

A word of warning - you should choose your accountability partners carefully because there are people who will not support you on your journey. When we set and start to achieve our running/training goals we change (for the better usually), and sometimes people close to you will not be able to handle the change and will; therefore, look to slow down or stop your progress. It's not unusual for some to encounter resistance from close friends and even partners, this is because they feel that if you change, then the friendship will not be the same and they just can't handle that.

For that very reason mentioned above, I recommend joining an established running group and sharing your goals with them. To add even more reason for you to achieve your long-term goal you might consider running a race of your chosen distance for a local charity. By seeing how you are helping others you will feel less selfish about yourself and the time you are spending training. This can be a big hurdle for beginners.

WHAT HAPPENS NEXT?

Well, now you work your socks off to make each target action happen either on or before your deadline. However, don't forget that your goals will change and evolve as you complete the process, so remain flexible in your thoughts and your approach. If a better possibility presents itself along the way, be prepared to change course and keep moving forward.

Start with two "easy fix"
short-term goals in order to build up
some confidence in the process.
1. Leave all training gear ready
to put on.
2. Organize all my post-workout needs
before every session.

At the start of each week, I would like you to review your goals and decide on some actions to take place for that week. Small actions on a regular basis are much more efficient and successful than something that you do just once in a while. Work smart and stay focused on your goals. Whoever you work for has goals set for you that will take up a lot of your waking time, but you must understand you are working for them and their greater good. On your own time, you are your boss, and the decisions and choices you make will shape your future.

With a little momentum, you will
start to challenge yourself with
bigger goals and targets.
Remember to treat a long-term large goal
like a series of short-term goals and
proceed one small step at a time.

Following this step-by-step process, you can view, analyze, and change any negative situation you are involved in, into a better one that can create new and compelling possibilities for yourself and your running. You are becoming the CEO of your own health and fitness company. You are starting to take control of your health and well-being. So, make decisions that will steer you in a positive direction and ultimately make you proud of yourself.

Remember – Your self-talk fuels your beliefs and behaviors and they in turn fuel your performance and results

PART 4: SMART NUTRITION

13: SMART NUTRITION OVERVIEW

It is essential that runners pay close attention to their food intake since everything we drink and eat has a direct impact on our performance and even our enjoyment of the sport: It can be hard to love running when you're feeling tired and sore from your last workout. So, I have a few quick tips for you to follow on how to fuel up for your runs, including the best energy sources and hydration strategies. Whether you're looking to improve your times or shed that final couple of pounds, the guidelines below will help make your mission more likely to succeed.

1. **Choose real foods over processed**

   The backbone of a runner's diet should consist predominantly of whole foods; most of which should be chicken and fish, vegetables, whole grains, nuts, low-fat dairy, and fruit. These healthy staples provide more nutritional value than the highly processed options that you can be tempted to go for if time is of the essence.

   Also, by taking the time to prepare your main meals at home, it allows you to have better control over your calorie intake. The consumption of convenience foods like energy gels during a run or a bottled smoothie afterward provide fast, nutritious fuel but should only be consumed occasionally and should be the exception rather than the norm.

If you're feeling hungry and it's not time to eat yet, drink a glass of water and wait 20 minutes. If you still feel hungry, then go and eat; otherwise, your body has alerted you to the fact that you are starting to dehydrate and lose energy.

2. **Choose good quality carbs**

   Carbohydrates are used to supply us with a quick energy source; and therefore, they go a long way to fueling your running workouts. They nourish tired muscles, and carbs should make up a large part of a runner's diet. But some carbs deliver greater value than others. It is best to make sure that most of your carbs are whole grains, fruits, and vegetables. The less processing any food source receives, the more nutritious it will be for you.

3. **Keep a diary**

   Although I do not want you to become obsessed with your running, while you are logging your training schedule it is a good idea to write down everything you eat and drink over a seven-day period, once every two months. This will help you to evaluate your eating habits. Are you snacking more than you realize? Reaching for sweets too often? By keeping an eye on your snacks, you will be able to identify areas where there's room for improvement.

4. **Everything in balance**

   Allow yourself the occasional treat. If you become obsessed with depriving yourself of the odd dessert, you will be less inclined to stick with the plan long-term. If you know you can have something sweet but choose not to have it, then you are in control and you will avoid establishing negative food choices and thought patterns. Just keep an eye on portion size and frequency.

5. **Stay hydrated**

   There is a lot more on this topic coming later, but for now, it is important to note that fluids are an essential part of any runner's diet. By staying correctly hydrated, you'll boost your performance and recovery times. But watch out for consuming idle calories. Still, water is by far your best option and be aware that drinks that are high in sugar can contribute to weight gain in a very sneaky way, over time. You should limit fruit juice to a minimum, pass on soft drinks totally, and switch your morning coffee to a cup of herbal tea. I especially like nettle tea and make sure you get plenty of water throughout the day.

AN ACIDIC SYSTEM IS A SICK SYSTEM

You need to keep acid levels in your body to a healthy balanced level. Acid can build up in your body through stress, food, drink, and exercise. If your body becomes over acidic, then your blood starts to get thicker and slows down. As it slows down, it can deposit materials like plaque and cholesterol in your arteries and this can lead to clotting, with a high risk of stroke and heart attack further down the road. It will also greatly slow down the delivery of oxygen to your muscles throughout the day and especially while exercising. The last thing you want is unnecessary levels of fatigue early on in your run.

The way to keep your acid levels under control is to continually work to gain an alkaline balance through your eating and drinking habits. For me, coffee is a big NO-NO. It dehydrates your body and then gives you a short uncontrollable rush of false energy while leaving you with a craving, or in some cases with an addiction.

Try to replace your coffee with herbal options like nettle tea, which will lower acidity or chamomiles which will relax your nervous system. Your daily food choices also play a large part in how your body deals with and neutralizes your acid levels. The more greens you can add to your diet the better.

14: THE IMPORTANCE OF WATER

When you get dehydrated,
the first things that suffer are your
motivation and your creativity.
Stay smart. Stay hydrated.
H2O all the way!

The first step and the quickest way to improve your health and vitality is to get and stay hydrated. A body is made up of 70% water. Most of us spend our day wandering around dehydrated trying to remember where we put our keys, or why we just ran up the stairs, or unable to remember someone's name and that's just before we leave the house.

As soon as your body starts to feel thirsty, you have already lost 20% of your available energy. By drinking water, you give yourself a much-needed energy boost, which will allow your brain to stay more alert and your body to break down toxins. Yes, drinking water is that simple and yet the benefits are massive.

WHY IS WATER SO IMPORTANT TO US?

To give you a quick insight how the body operates when we are fully hydrated, we need to understand the movement of our four main electrolytes: sodium, potassium, calcium and magnesium. These electrolytes actually charge the body. In other words, they give us energy. As the electrolytes move through their daily cycle, they have a big effect on our body. They affect our energy levels and mood patterns. In a fully hydrated person, this means they have the ability to freely carry messages and signals around the body.

So, any negative movement of these significant electrolytes can lead us to feel tired at the end of a busy day, but if you make sure that you are well hydrated you will lessen the effects of this chemical action on your body. So, improve your moods and your energy levels by remaining hydrated.

Lymph fluid is generally similar to blood plasma except that it also contains white blood cells. Lymph fluid returns proteins and excess interstitial fluid to the bloodstream. Lymph fluid also picks up bacteria and brings them to lymph nodes where they are destroyed. Lymph fluid transports fats from the digestive system and is an important waste disposal system for the body. It then carries the waste matter away from the cells and into one of the other major cleaning systems of the body. When this process is complete, you have the perfect exchange of fluids and electrolytes, and you end up with nice clean cells and a nice healthy body.

WHAT HAPPENS WHEN WE ARE DEHYDRATED?

Our body will never work against us and it will always, without exception, do the very best it can for us at any given point in time. So, when we are dehydrated it will protect us, but what happens if we ignore the signals our body is sending us? We move into a negative state where our ability to motivate oneself and be creative is greatly reduced. We stop moving forward because we are under attack and we have to move into survival mode. This means that all unnecessary body functions are suspended. This is not good for us.

Imagine if you were to spend 70% of your life in a state of dehydration. Can you see what the real consequences might potentially be? Most people will survive in a semi-dehydrated state, but we want to thrive. In a sports capacity, where the demands on the body and its output are far greater than the normal pace we live at, we must be hydrated at all times.

WHY DON'T PEOPLE DRINK MORE WATER?

The main reason why people don't drink enough water is that they don't understand the value of water and the effects of dehydration on their system. There are very few ads on TV and radio telling you "to drink more water." The short list below is an insight into how water can help with some of the issues many people face on a daily basis that could be greatly improved by increasing water intake.

WATER AND "ADULT ONSET DIABETES"

Adult onset diabetes (Type 2 Diabetes) can be brought on as a result of dehydration and in time can cause massive damage to the blood vessels all over the body. It may eventually cause the loss of toes, feet, and legs from gangrene.

It is critical to have adequate water supply circulating throughout our bodies for the brain to perform its task of thinking, decision-making, prioritization, focus, and to keep us safe. In diabetes, only some cells get the bare amount of water to survive. So, adequate water consumption can help prevent adult onset diabetes.

WATER CAN HELP TO LOWER BLOOD CHOLESTEROL

High Cholesterol levels are an indicator of early drought management in the body. Cholesterol is a clay-like material that is poured into the gaps of some cell membranes to safeguard them from losing their vital water content to the more powerful blood circulating in their vicinity. As well as being used to manufacture nerve cell membranes and hormones, cholesterol is also used as a shield against water transference from other vital cells that would normally exchange water through their cell membranes.

When your body becomes dehydrated and the cells start to lose their water content, the body recognizes the need to preserve water in the cell. This causes the manufacture and release of cholesterol. Once there is a high level of cholesterol in the body it starts to stick to the arterial walls and this causes blockages in blood circulation. These blockages can lead to clots and these clots can lead to strokes and heart attacks. I am not suggesting that you manage your cholesterol levels solely with water, but it can help to slow the manufacture and release of negative cholesterol into the arteries.

Note: It is very important that you keep a close eye on your cholesterol levels. Even if your food intake is good, it is possible to inherit a condition of high cholesterol. So, everyone should get their cholesterol levels checked by a medical professional regularly.

WATER CAN HELP PREVENT ARTHRITIS

Arthritis is a sign of water shortage in the painful joint. This is true for people of any age.

Drink plenty of water and take more than usual when you are training. The water will have a very positive effect on your ability to perform and you will recover quicker than otherwise. It's a very simple change to make in your life and one that you should carry with you for the rest of your life.

I hope by now I have convinced you that we need to make sure that we are getting the correct quantity of water for our body and mind to function at its optimum level.

To calculate your optimal daily water intake, visit

www.Quantumflowperformance.com/runningbook to download your free guide to better hydration. It will take the guesswork out of the art of drinking enough water each day. You may find that it is more than you are used to, but most people simply don't drink enough water. Because hunger and thirst send similar signals and feelings to our body, we often mistake hunger for thirst.

The formula is based on a person not undertaking an exercise regime. So, if you are exercising (and you should be) then more water is required.

YOUR HOMEWORK

First, calculate your daily water optimum intake using the formula.
Go to **www.Quantumflowperformance.com/runningbook** to access it and then make sure you achieve or surpass that figure daily without fail. By all means, share this information with your accountability partner so you stay on track, and it will help them also become motivated to be more hydrated on a daily basis just like you. This action will be sure to improve their health and vitality as well as yours.

15: WHY RUNNERS SHOULD DETOX

Some people take great care in looking after their cars, their motorcycles, and even their sports equipment, but when it comes to looking after their own body, they are very reluctant to keep it clean and lubricated. We need to clean out our "engines" on a regular basis.

While I understand that you are reading this book from a running perspective, we have to take into consideration the fact that our bodies build up waste products over time, and it becomes saturated and can no longer do its job properly, resulting in sickness. This toxic waste can make us feel tired and sore, so we need to agree to get as much waste out of our body as possible on a continuous basis. Otherwise, it will take us longer to recover and we will not get the most energy from our routine.

The three keys to getting the optimum from your diet is to regularly Cleanse, Nourish, and Balance your systems.

The first stage in getting your body in optimal shape is to cleanse (or empty out) the "waste basket in your body." Then you can move into the nourishing stage which provides the energy you need to flush out the toxins and finally, you can move into the balancing stage where you will restore harmony to your systems.

These detox systems should only be done once a year, but an effort to do the routine twice a year should be considered. The order in which we cleanse our systems is very simple. You should start from the bottom and work up; so its colon, kidney, and then liver.

Our body does most of its best cleansing and repair work at night, so it is important to always try to get a good night's sleep.

THE COLON

I always recommend the best place to start this internal cleansing operation is in the colon. There is no point in clearing out other systems if everything just gets backed up on the final leg of its journey. So, to avoid complications, make sure the first part of any routine cleanse is all about the exit door!

THE COLON CLEANSE

The best way to gently clean the colon is to take half a teaspoon of baking soda and a shot of water first thing in the morning and the last thing at night for five days. Then, take a break for five days and repeat this sequence for a total of three sets. This will have two effects on your body, but the main one is that you will greatly reduce the acid levels in your body while cleaning out the stubborn debris from your colon.

Once you have successfully completed your colon cleanse you can move on to the kidney and liver and other cleanses.

THE KIDNEY

The kidneys are two bean shaped organs. They are each the size of the owner's fist. They are located towards the back of the body and just below the rib cage. There is one on each side of the spine. Our two kidneys filter between 120 to 150 quarts of blood and this produces about 1 to 2 liters of urine, every day over a 24-hour period.

Our kidneys are used to clean and dissolve any water-soluble toxins from our blood and if the filters in our kidneys are blocked, we can expect a decrease in our blood quality. This over time will lead to us having less ability to transport oxygen around our bodies. This ultimately means we will have less energy and a slower recovery time from exercise.

THE KIDNEY CLEANSE

The easiest way to clean your kidneys is to increase your intake of water through a 24-hour period. If you have no specific medical conditions or dietary needs, then you might consider taking a break from heavier proteins, carbohydrates, and sugars and moving over to a lighter diet for about 3 days. Just consuming raw fruit and vegetables as well as water rich foods, with plenty of water will give your kidneys enough time and extra energy to clean its filters.

THE LIVER

Your liver plays a large part in how you move and feel. It can become overburdened with toxins and slow its cleaning system down until it starts to feel hard to the touch and has no room to move. There are some fascinating links between the liver and sports performance. It is important to consider the health of yours very carefully.

For example, reduced mobility in the right shoulder can be caused by tension being inferred from the large triangular ligament which divides the right and left liver lobes. If the ligament has been strained or impacted upon, then it will pull the shoulder forward and down also reducing your lung capacity, which will decrease performance potential.

THE LIVER CLEANSE IN 2 DAYS

Start the Liver cleanse with a light no fat breakfast and take no medication, vitamins, or pills that you can do without.

Do not eat after 2:00 pm. This allows the bile to build up in the liver and develop pressure to push out any small blockages. Now get your Epsom salts ready. Mix 4 tbsp. in 3 cups of water and pour it into a jar. This makes 4 serving cups. Now place in the fridge to chill. This will improve the taste:

- **Day 1**
  Watermelon and grapes for breakfast.
  For the rest of the day only eat raw or cooked vegetables.
- **Day 2**
  Vegetable juice only.
  At 9:00 pm, take 2 Fl. OZ. of olive oil and 2 Fl. OZ. of lemon juice.
  Repeat every 15 minutes - 4 times in total.

On the last time you take the mixture, you should retire to bed and lay on your right side.

Drink plenty of fluid both days - water and herbal teas.

Fennel can also help to cleanse the Liver and detoxify the body.

Always do your kidney cleanse before you do your liver cleanse.

If you decide to go ahead with any of these cleansing recommendations, then there are a couple of things you should know about each.

Firstly, the colon cleanse. There are plenty of different types of baking soda available. I would recommend that you get a good quality one that is aluminum free. Mix the baking soda in warm (pre-boiled and cooled water) and drink immediately. You can expect a medium aftertaste, but everyone has different tolerance levels, and I personally find it just about acceptable. This will have the effect of a looser bowel than normal so make sure you have access to a bathroom. Start this cleanse on your first day off and make sure you have nothing planned so you can react in comfort to any demands that your body might make on you. You should not experience any major discomfort; however, we are all different and it is always best to prepare for the worst and expect the best. After just a few days you will start to feel lighter, fresher, and have more energy.

The Kidney detox plan is very gentle on the body. There are no hidden challenges to deal with or prepare for in my experience. Fruit and vegetables with plenty of water for about 3 days will give your kidneys the time and power to clear most of the filter blockages and restore normal services.

This type of diet will also support the colon cleanse that you also completed recently.

You will have to plan a little better for the Liver cleanse. With just 48 hours of light food required, you are in the perfect place diet-wise to move straight from your kidney cleanse to the liver cleanse. At this stage of your cleanse, your bowel may be a little loose, but that's to be expected. The whole idea is to clean out your systems, and the best way for your body to eliminate large waste matter and fat-soluble toxins are via the colon. So, just be aware of what might happen and construct your appointments accordingly.

Once your detox is complete, I would recommend taking a good quality probiotic for about six weeks to make sure you also have a healthy gut and digestive system in order to take advantage of the key organs you have just cleaned out.

I love to juice, and my favorite combination is very simple to make and very tasty as well. When I first started juicing many years ago the juicing machines were very awkward and cumbersome not to mention difficult to clean out after use. Now they are easy to use and quick to clean, but if that's still not enough to make you buy one you should be able to locate a juice bar near you and try to consume a juice at least four times per week.

JUICE

2 Carrots

Large handful of Spinach

1 Celery stick (with leaves)

2 Apples

LYMPHATIC SYSTEM

While the major organ cleanses should be an annual occurrence in your health schedule, maintaining an active flow with your lymphatic system is crucial. It is one of the most important systems in the body and works tirelessly to keep the body healthy and free from disease.

The lymphatic system consists of the lymph vessels and nodes, tonsils, adenoids, appendix, spleen, and thymus gland. These are all the organs and tissues that provide much of the body's natural defenses to sickness and disease. The lymph vessels carry lymph fluid, which transports the majority of the toxins and waste away from the body's tissues and organs, to the veins under the collarbones, where the fluid then enters the bloodstream. The waste is eventually filtered out of the body by the liver and kidneys.

Unlike the circulatory system, the lymphatic system has no pump to move its fluid around, which means that it is entirely dependent on movement and exercise to keep it detoxing and cleansing the body to the best of its ability. Muscle movement effectively squeezes the lymph vessels to shift lymph fluid towards the subclavian veins close to the heart, and deep breathing squeezes the lymphatic thoracic duct, which pours most of the body's lymph into the bloodstream.

SKIN BRUSHING AND IMPROVING LYMPH FLOW

Skin brushing is also a great way to improve lymph flow and help the body to deal with water retention. This technique is performed by using a skin brush in an upward direction always moving towards the heart on a daily basis.

- Start at the toes and use long upward strokes.
- Brush each part of the body for about 4 to 6 strokes.
- No need to brush too hard.
- Also try this Juice daily for 3 Weeks, to improve lymph flow.

LYMPH FLOW JUICE

2 apples

1 lemon

piece of ginger

3 cups of grapes

16: GETTING FUELLED UP

You are what you eat. Period! When it comes to eating well and reaping the rewards both on and off your daily battlefield, a small amount of planning and discipline will take you a long way towards making the physical improvements you desire. All you need to do is get your food intake in order. The trick is not to stress about your food and remember you can pre-empt most tricky food situations by planning ahead and being organized. Your discipline starts in the supermarket. If you don't want to be tempted, then just don't buy it. There is always a healthy option just around the corner in the next aisle.

Most people are good at making healthy choices for their main meals, but when it comes to snack time, we are a mess. Spoiled for choice and looking for a quick fix, this is when our hunger demons surface and tempt us with sayings like "it's just one," and "there is nothing else to eat," or "I don't have time." In order to help yourself in avoiding these food choice dilemmas, prepare yourself with sensible food options ahead of time. If you like a snack, just stash a few healthy snacks in accessible areas like an office drawer, your bag or car, and of course at home.

Have a healthy snack before you go out for a meal. This will leave you less dependent on the menu and take some pressure off. Otherwise, you may be starving and overeat.

Being able to create a healthy meal strategy is very important. Here are a few tips you can employ to keep you on the right track:

1. Drink plenty of water. This will be repeated again and again. It is that important!
2. Your intake of carbohydrate must be relative to your activity level.
3. Choose carbs that are rich in fiber e.g. sweet potatoes, green peas, apples.
4. Take a lean source of protein with each main meal.
5. Eating smaller portions more often through the day is best.
6. Try to mix your food types for nutritional value and variety.
7. Eat a healthy breakfast each morning.
8. Add a multivitamin and an antioxidant to your routine.
9. Drink a "post-workout" shake after your exercise.
10. Cut out sugar wherever possible and be aware of the hidden sugars.

Make simple changes like drink water, not fizzy drinks and consume herbal teas, not regular tea and/or coffee. Eat plenty of fresh salads and stay away from pork as it is full of acid.

If you are looking to cut down on the number of calories you take in, then the best thing to do is to cut them out of your drinks as well. Try to replace your soft fizzy drinks and juices with water. Without the calories to burn from the fizzy drinks, your body will start to burn the quality carbs you are eating for energy. This should lead to fat loss and weight loss more rapidly than when your body is fighting against itself with your consumption of soda and juice calories.

Nowadays many people have a juice or smoothie maker in the house. Start making your own smoothies and fresh juices. Don't be afraid to experiment with different flavor combinations. For a fraction of the cost of juice bars, you can create simple and delicious energy boosting, body cleansing drinks that will support your nutritional needs on a daily basis. These juices are packed with goodness and are a great way to help you lower acid levels in your body. Remember an acidic system is a sick system.

Timing your food intake around your workout is most important. If you eat too close to a training session, you will most likely develop cramps, feel full and sluggish, and more than likely not be able to perform at your highest level. Getting the right food at the right time is the key to keeping the body well-nourished while training. Timing your meals and snacks will help to regulate blood sugar levels and provide the body with a fuel source that will keep you energized all day.

SAMPLE MENU FOR A RUNNING SCHEDULE

Try this option if you are planning a Lunchtime Workout:

7:30 am: Breakfast – Oatmeal or Muesli with Berries

10:00 am: Snack

11:45 am: Apple or a pre-workout shake

12:30 pm: Workout

1:30 pm: Lunch – Chicken fillet with brown bread and Salad or Raw Veg

4:00 pm: Snack – Shake

7:00 pm: Dinner – Grill lean red meat with brown rice and vegetables.

10:00 pm: Snack – no sugar

Or, this option is suitable if you are planning an Evening Workout:

07:30 am: Breakfast – Oatmeal or Muesli with Berries

10:30 am: Snack

1:00 pm: Lunchtime – Chicken with raw spinach and tomatoes with nuts and olive oil

4:00 pm: Snack

6:00 pm: Dinner – Fresh fish with vegetables

7:30 pm: Workout

9:30 pm: Snack | Shake – no sugar

Your body takes 48 hours to react to diet changes. Correct food and drink choices on Thursdays and Fridays will positively impact your energy levels during your weekend events.

17: TARGETED SUPPLEMENTS

It is a well-known fact that most of us do not get enough nutrition from our daily food intake. It can be difficult to get the right balance of vitamins and minerals from our meals and snacks in what can be a fast-paced lifestyle. Being able to not only cope but thrive within this fast-paced lifestyle takes a lot of effort and planning. As the seasons progress, the demands on your body adjusts; and therefore, your nutritional needs change. On top of that, if you add in your training schedules and the amount of energy and repair required to fuel your training and competition schedule, it is not surprising that many "healthy" athletes become ill at the most inopportune times (i.e. the day of or a few days before a big event).

As an experienced health practitioner and a runner, I decided to put my own range of supplements together. I was not happy with the generalized approach to targeting body systems. There are so many conflicting reports as to which supplements are the best and so many options to choose from. It is very easy for people to become misinformed and misled. You end up spending unnecessarily large amounts of hard earned cash on products that are not giving you the best return for your money.

We all have different needs due to our diet preferences/goals and all supplements do different things. Most supplements contain large amounts of synthetically manufactured ingredients. I prefer to keep it simple and natural whenever possible.

When you are taking multiple sources of supplements or even a multivitamin supplement on a daily basis, there are going to be certain ingredients in the product that you do not need. Then it is up to your liver and kidneys to sort out the toxic waste. If you are already feeling tired from daily life, the extra effort you have to put into clearing the toxins will only make you even more tired. And so, the cycle will continue.

I think that the most efficient form of supplementation is one that supports or enhances an important organ, system, or function in the body such as the heart, lungs, liver etc. When you focus on enhancing the correct systems in the body, you get multiple positive results without the downside of overworking the liver and kidneys.

Having the ability to counterbalance the negative effects that stress has on your body holds a massive advantage for any person involved in an exercise schedule.

Two of the most obvious health issues we face at the moment are heart disease and the impact that stress has on us over a sustained period. We can be very aware of heart and circulation problems because they can be accurately measured over time, but stress lurks in the shadows until a major negative health event happens and forces us to take a close look at our lifestyle.

Nowadays it is possible to address these issues through supplementation and this has a very positive impact on the rest of our body functions at the same time. In essence it is possible for us to support the daily function and repair of our cardiovascular system and our immune system with the correct supplementation to our current nutrition intake.

As I mentioned in the introduction, the two products that I would highly recommend for Runners and all who take regular exercise, are "All Day Energy" and "SportMax." Each of these products works to enhance and support a critical system in the body (such as the cardiovascular system and immune system amongst others) to provide energy and repair at the same time. As a result of nourishing specific organs and glands, you gain improved function of all other body systems and the overall results are dramatic.

ADRENAL FATIGUE

Our adrenal glands are pressed into action every time we encounter stress. They produce adrenaline for us at times of intense physical exertion and during stressful situations. The adrenalin then binds to our muscles to make them stronger and that, in turn, helps us to cope with increased levels of physical demands on our bodies in the short-term.

When we need to sustain this high level of physical output for long periods, our adrenal glands cannot maintain their production levels of adrenalin and we start producing the chemical Cortisol. This is not as powerful as adrenalin, but it stays in the blood stream a lot longer. It is; however, corrosive to our Hippocampus which located in our brain. One of its functions is memory recall.

Our adrenal glands are not just used at times of physical exertion; they are also fired up when stress comes into our lives. If you are running long distances and enduring high levels of stress on a regular basis, you are likely to overuse your adrenal glands, and this can potentially lead to adrenal fatigue.

If you have the perception that you have a stressful job, then you do. It is likely that your adrenal glands are working overtime on a daily basis and you may not even realize it. You see, once our fight or flight sequence is activated we can't stop the process, not even if we realize that the situation is a false alarm. So, we are registering both real stress and false stress as the same thing and both situations have the exact same effect on our bodies.

Adrenalin surges into our muscles, we lose access to the frontal part of our brain (where we make our rational assessments of situations) and we are given only two options - fight or flight. If a stressful situation arrives when you are at work or interacting with your family and friends, it is likely that it will be recognizable in the form of aggression. Because we have lost temporary access to our frontal brain, we might end up saying or doing something we might regret later.

When our adrenals glands are overworked, our liver also becomes overworked. It has to clean up the excess toxins floating around in the bloodstream that stress related chemicals cause. Our liver produces an important antioxidant called Glutathione. This helps to counteract the damage that "free radicals" cause and without this antioxidant the free radicals float around bumping into cell walls causing serious damage. The most visibly obvious effect to the naked eye is premature ageing; but if you nourish, repair, and support the adrenal glands they will happily look after you and indirectly keep you looking younger. That's why people with less stress in their lives look younger.

The best way you can repair adrenal fatigue is to take a premium quality zinc supplement and eat a balanced diet. Another indirect effect of possible adrenal fatigue is poor energy levels and a tendency to store belly fat. So, if you ignore small daily stressful situation (real or imaginary) you may just be heading for premature ageing, excess belly fat, hypertension, and a mid-life crisis.

CASE STUDY

When you put this information into a case study, you may recognize symptoms of someone you might know - maybe even yourself. I will use "John" as my case study, but I could just as easily use "Joanne."

- Male
- Age 38
- IT Consultant
- Full-time job / Studying part-time

- 2 children under the age of 10

The average day for John starts out with a 6:45 A. M. alarm call. Quick shower, some breakfast, makes his children's lunches for the day and out of the house to make the 45-minute commute to his office by car. Traffic is always busy, especially as he gets closer to the city center where he works. The last 20 minutes of his journey is particularly challenging and frustrating, mainly due to other commuters not obeying the rules of the road and many of them taking silly risks - including the cyclists and pedestrians. He arrives to work mildly anxious but dismisses the feeling as normal and gets straight to work.

A new project had been assigned to him ten days ago and with a possible promotion on the horizon, he is keen to show the boss that he is well capable. The deadline date for the project completion is looming and one of John's more experienced colleagues is out sick for a couple of days while he attends the hospital for some tests. John decides to start working through lunch at his desk and stays a bit later in the evenings to keep the project on track.

The commute home is not so bad except his head is filled with solving the work problems that had occurred that day. At home he has a healthy dinner and catches up with his family for an hour, and then it's time for study. An assignment is due next week, and he is getting a little stressed as he is finding it hard to grasp some of the course material. Some extra study time would be required to pass the assignment.

He runs upstairs to say goodnight to his children and goes straight back to the books. His partner is very supportive, and although they also work, they are finding the schedule of joint family commitments is being passed over by John.

And that's just an average day.

I think we can all see where this is going to end up. Varying amounts of stress absorbed by both adults in the relationship on a daily basis will lead to loss of appetite, poor moods, and low tolerance levels. These symptoms cause even more stress and the problems escalate from there. Any time there is high levels of sustainable stress involved you can expect your immune system to become weakened and physical illness to follow. The subsequent overuse of the adrenal glands can cause issues in the liver and kidneys which can, in turn, lead to Chronic Fatigue Syndrome and other serious problems.

So, supplements are not the only answer to the situation above. It is clear that taking regularly scheduled breaks, eating correct nutrition, and maintaining a healthy work/life balance are all very important. It has been well proven that zinc can play a large part in nourishing both the Adrenal glands and boosting the immune system. Oysters happen to be the highest source of natural zinc available and when you couple that with the other 59 trace elements, 19 amino acids, and 12 vitamins which they provide, Oysters can offer us a great amount of energy and improved mental focus during the day. That's why I chose these shellfish as my number one supplement for active people.

If we take the case study above and increase the age of John by eight years, we can see how his symptoms have changed. He has finished his extra study course and qualified with distinction. He also got promoted. His children are thinking about going to college. His office workload is a little different, but there are still high levels of stress involved now that he is directly responsible for a small team and the successful outcome of several high-end accounts. He starts to become uncomfortable in groups and family gatherings, and his partner notices that he has gained weight, developed a short temper and in essence, has lost his mojo. He finds out that there is a hereditary issue of heart disease in his family and he correctly arranges a doctor's appointment. He has recently been placed on medication for both high cholesterol and high blood pressure. He is finding it hard to get used to taking the medication and has started skipping it because it makes him feel different and uncomfortable. If you recognize this pattern of events, then I recommend you get yourself straight down to your doctor and explain your symptoms ASAP.

Welcome to a mid-life crisis. In a nutshell, your brain is telling you that you should look and feel younger, but your body can't cope.

John can't believe that only a few short years ago he was a fit, healthy thirty-year-old who played on his college basketball team and was able to mix it up on the court with some of his pals until his career and family responsibilities got in the way - where did it all go wrong?

My advice is to forget about the past. Look at the lifestyle path you took to get here. Take stock of all the negative stress that was endured and set up a plan to take you out of the desperate health issues that you will face if you continue the way you are. Develop a new lifestyle routine

Nutrition and correct supplementation are also going to play a large part in your recovery because they provide much needed energy. The SportsMax supplement formula, based on the incredible work of Nobel Laureate, Dr. L. Ignarro. It is designed to improve circulation in your body, facilitating the ability to deliver more fuel to muscles to help you perform better during exercise, and also repair muscle faster after exercise.

Our bodies make a chemical called Nitric Oxide during exercise and at certain times of our sleep cycle. As we get older, we make less Nitric Oxide and do less intense exercise, thus creating less Nitric Oxide. Nitric Oxide tones our arteries. In other words, it keeps them flexible and as we get older, we tend to lose the arterial flexibility that we enjoyed in our youth.

The ingredients in SportsMax are designed to create a natural spike in the production of NO. Not only does it help to tone our arteries the knock-on effects are significant. It can also help to reduce cholesterol levels while stabilizing blood pressure. With improved circulation, you will also be able to support all your organs, glands, and muscles; therefore, leading to improve your all-around health.

STRESS

The biggest challenge that John (our case study) faces is undetected stress. You see, the word "stress" has lost its power of meaning and we are now getting used to being told that a certain amount of stress is good for us. While that may well be the case you can never predict just how much stress a situation will cause you and how much is good for you. Equally we are all different; and therefore, have different tolerance levels of stress. Exercise and in particular running is a great way to release tension from your muscles. Stress/tension build up in the muscles is the very reason why you should take time to warm up properly before every session. To help us maintain and build healthy muscles we must pay close attention to our diet and nutrition.

It is a well-known fact that most of us do not get enough nutrition from our daily food intake. It can be difficult to get the right balance of vitamins and minerals from our meals and snacks in what can be a fast-paced lifestyle. Being able to not only cope but thrive within this fast-paced lifestyle takes a lot of effort and planning. When you take into consideration the fact that as the seasons' progress, the demands on your body adjusts; and therefore, your nutritional needs change. On top of that, if you add in your training schedules and the amount of energy and repair required to fuel your training and competition schedule, it is not surprising that many "healthy" athletes become ill at the most inopportune times (i.e. the day of or a few days before a big event).

One of the most widely acknowledged causes of illness is stress. This feeling of stress can arrive anywhere - from over-training, to a missed deadline or a relationship problem, to bad food choices, but all these issues have one thing in common.

Yes, you guessed it; they all build up stress in your body.

The best way to describe the internal negative effects of stress on the body is that it compresses and restricts the fluid movement of all your muscles, organs, and glands. This stress causes oxidative damage, especially in the mitochondria of your cells. The mitochondria are known as the energy power plant of your cells. Stress directly affects the mitochondria causing the cells to produce less energy. Symptoms include fatigue, compromised immunity, premature ageing, and reduced libido.

18: GETTING BACK ON THE WAGON

Because life is full of pitfalls and excuses, you need to have a few quick fixes in case you fall away from the path of health and fitness. You can choose from a range of holistic options below as to how you are going to restore balance to your body. Please make sure that you use these techniques with the same amount of passion and commitment that you showed when you were falling off the wagon.

- Exercise and movement coupled with deep breathing are the best way to restore balance to your body. So get moving and deep breathing as soon as you can.

- Exercises like the "Saw" (number 6 in the Stability Exercises), "Bow and Arrow" and the "Two-Way Spine Stretch" (numbers 2 and 8 in in the Recovery Exercises) will all activate the liver and spleen, which will boost your immune system and flush toxins fast.

- If you don't have time immediately to exercise the next morning or a gentler approach is required, then please start by drinking more water.

- Skin brush daily to improve lymph flow. This is best done in the morning before a shower. Always use long strokes and move toward the heart. Start at the feet and work up the body.

Also try this Juice daily to improve lymph flow (to be taken every day for 3 weeks):

- 2 apples / 1 lemon / piece of ginger / 3 cups of grapes

OR

- Take 1/4 tsp of cayenne pepper in a small amount of Organic Cider Vinegar 3 times per week for 3 weeks. This will help to clear the bloodstream.
- Start back with your exercise plan as soon as possible.
- Cut out Tea / Coffee / Chocolate / Alcohol / White bread.
- Start to lower the Acid Levels in your body by taking a bath with a mug of Epsom salts dissolved in it.
- Drink Herbal Teas: Nettle or Green.
- Take Spirulina or wheatgrass.
- Eat fruit only on an empty stomach.
- Eat lots of raw veg as snacks and put in salads.
- Introduce nuts and seeds to your diet.
- Keep at least 1 day as a Vegetarian day each week.
- Use breath work to help to detoxify and stimulate the body.

To dissolve indigestion this week, take teaspoon of baking soda in a shot of warm water, morning and evening for 5 days.

PART 5: APPENDICES

APPENDIX I: QUICK START PLAN

28 DAY EXERCISE AND RUNNING PLAN

WEEK 1

Day 01: Warm-up Routine – 10 min walk / 3 min jog / 10 min walk / Recovery exercises

Day 02: Warm-up + Stability exercises / Recovery exercises

Day 03: Rest

Day 04: Warm-up – 10min walk / 3 min jog / 8 min walk / 2 min jog / Recovery exercises

Day 05: Warm- up + Stability exercises – 10 min walk / 3 min jog / 8 min walk / 2 min jog / Recovery exercises

Day 06: Rest

Day 07: Warm-up – 10min walk / 3min jog / 7min walk / 3min jog / Recovery exercises

WEEK 2

Day 08: Warm-up + Stability exercises – 5 min walk / 4 min jog / 5 min walk / 4 min jog / Recovery exercises

Day 09: Rest

Day 10: Warm-up – 5 min walk / 7 min jog / 3 min walk / 5 min jog / 5 min walk / Recovery exercises.

Day 11: Warm-up + Stability exercises – 3 min walk / 8 min jog / 3 min walk / 5 min jog / Recovery exercises

Day 12: Rest

Day 13: Warm-up + Stability exercises – 2 min walk / 10 min jog / 2 min walk / 5 min jog / Recovery exercises

Day 14: Warm-up + Stability exercises – 2 min walk / 10 min jog / 2 min walk / 6 min jog / Recovery exercises

WEEK 3

Day 15: Rest

Day 16: Warm-up + Stability exercises – 2 min walk / 14 min jog / 2 min jog / 6 min jog / 2 min walk / Recovery exercises.

Day 17: Warm-up – 2 min walk / 16 min jog / 2 min walk / 6 min jog / 1 min walk / Recovery exercise

Day 18: Rest

Day 19: Warm-up + Stability exercises – 2 min walk / 16 min jog / 2 min walk / 8 min jog / 2 min walk / Recovery exercises

Day 20: Warm-up – 2 min walk / 20 min jog / 2 min walk / 6 min jog / 2 min walk / Recovery exercises

Day 21: Rest

WEEK 4

Day 22: Warm-up + Stability exercises – 1 min walk / 22 min jog / 2 min walk / 6 min jog / 1 min walk / Recovery exercises

Day 23: Warm-up + Stability exercises – 1 min walk / 25 min jog / 2 min walk / Recovery

Day 24: Rest

Day 25: Warm-up / 1 min walk / 26 min jog / 2 min walk / Recovery exercises

Day 26: Warm-up + Stability exercises / 1 min walk / 26 min jog / 2 min walk / Recovery exercises

Day 27: Rest

Day 28: Warm-up - 1 min walk / 30 min jog / 2 min walk / Recovery exercises

---

If you have tired feet at the end of the week, try soaking them in warm water and 1/2 mug of Epsom salts for 10min.

APPENDIX II: HEALTHY FOODS

LOW GLYCEMIC ALKALINE FOODS

FRUITS
Apples, Pears, Passion Fruit, Melons, Kiwis, Fresh Apricots, Gooseberries, Cherries, Dates, Grapes, Limes and Mangos.

VEGETABLES
Broccoli, Brussels Sprouts, Cabbage, Carrots, Cauliflower, Cucumber, Zucchini, Fresh Ginger, Peppers, Rhubarb, Spinach and Turnips.

GRAINS
Millet, Wild Rice

BEANS
Chickpeas, Kidney Beans, Lentils, Peas, all soya products

NUTS+SEEDS
Brazil Nuts, Sesame Seed, Almonds, Chestnuts

OILS
Fish Oils, Almond Oil, Avocado Oil and Sunflower Oil.

MEDIUM GLYCEMIC ALKALINE FOODS

FRUIT
Pineapple, Strawberries

VEGETABLE
Sweetcorn

GRAINS
Wholemeal Pasta, Wholemeal Bread, Brown Rice, Oats and

Puffed Rice

SEEDS
Pumpkin Seeds and Sunflower Seeds.

DAIRY
Skimmed Milk and Dairy free milk e.g.: Soya or Rice Milk.

HIGH GLYCAEMIC ALKALINE FOODS

FRUIT
Bananas and Dried Fruit.

VEGETABLES
White Potatoes and Parsnips.

SUGARS
Honey and Syrup.

ACID-FORMING FOODS

FRUITS
Plums, Prunes Tomatoes, Cranberries and Citrus Fruits.

DAIRY PRODUCTS
Butter, Cheese, Custard, Cream and Full-fat Yoghurts.

GRAINS
White Bread, White Pasta, Basmati Rice, Popcorn, Pastries, Cakes and Biscuits.

NUTS
Peanuts, Pecans, Walnuts, Macadamias, Cashew Nuts and Pistachios.

OTHERS
All processed foods, Red Meats, Chocolate, Tea and Coffee.

POST-TRAINING MEAL

Post-exercise snacks should be high in carbohydrates with a

smaller amount of protein. This will replace the carbohydrates burned during the exercise session and start the muscle fiber repairing process. Refueling is most effective almost immediately after your exercise session. This will avoid fatigue and the onset of overtraining.

Large Banana or Apple

3 Fig Rolls

700ml Isotonic sports drink

Water

A combination of healthy eating and a good exercise plan will improve general health, exercise performance, and help you reach your goals. The list of foods below should be taken in moderation. There are plenty of alternatives that can be put in the shopping trolley.

YOUR HOMEWORK

Follow these healthy tips for home dining:

1. To make a meal, combine protein and one or two vegetables.
2. Once a day, combine protein and carbohydrates.
3. Eat regular smaller portion meals.
4. Consume at least 3 liters of water throughout the day.
5. Eat low glycemic foods i.e.: Fruit first thing in the morning.
6. Eat slowly and enjoy your food.
7. Do not skip meals or let yourself get weak with hunger.
8. Steam, bake or grill foods, do not fry!
9. Steam vegetables, vitamins, and minerals are lost through boiling.

10. Use low-fat salad dressing.
11. Do not use Mayonnaise or salad cream.
12. Add black pepper to foods instead of salt to enhance flavor.

I prefer to keep it natural and work in harmony with the body. Only see supplements as just that and not as a replacement for healthy eating.

APPENDIX III: SUPPLEMENTS

Quantum Flow Performance "All Day Energy" is made in Ireland. This product owes all its fantastic natural health-giving properties to the clean, fresh Atlantic waters off the beautiful West Coast of Ireland and the bountiful supply of high-quality Fresh Oysters it provides.

The reason why Oysters have been so highly prized through the centuries is because of their power to: increase energy levels, slow down the ageing process, and offset the symptoms of fatigue and stress while boosting the immune system. They can also help you to maintain strong levels of collagen and keratin production for faster wound and injury healing as well as forming healthier hair, skin, and nails.

WHAT MAKES THIS PRODUCT DIFFERENT TO OTHER ENERGY SUPPLEMENTS?

One of the key reasons why this product can deliver all these amazing benefits is because Oysters have the ability to stimulate the natural production of Glutathione in your body. Research has shown that raised Glutathione levels decrease muscle damage, reduce recovery time, increase strength and endurance, and shifts metabolism from fat production to muscle development. The benefits of this little known but massively important Antioxidant are mind blowing, and in my opinion are vital for living an energized healthy lifestyle. This product is also jam packed with many other natural and essential daily vitamins and minerals including quality fish oils EPA and DHA, 59 trace elements, 19 amino acids, and 12 vitamins.

It can help you overcome fatigue and tiredness. People who exercise, endurance athletes, stressed out professionals, individuals who are exposed to environmental stresses such as UV light, smoking, and alcohol all suffer from higher than normal levels of oxidative stress and free radical build up. The fatigue and tiredness associated with the higher than normal levels of oxidative stress from these pursuits have been shown to decrease by taking "All Day Energy." It can also help to slow down the ageing process and improve skin conditions. You see, free radical damage is one of the major causes of premature ageing in tissues, especially the skin. This cellular damage, mainly due to exercising in the outdoors, has led to the phrase "Runners Face." Free radical damage in the cells also reduces the cell's ability to produce energy and leads to overall loss of vitality and endurance. Clinical human trials on All Day Energy have shown that after just 8 days, oxidative stress in the blood was reduced by 90%. This proves that All Day Energy has great potential to help reduce the causes of premature ageing.

All Day Energy also promotes tissue repair, has an anti-inflammatory effect, and contains the building blocks for the enzymes, which destroy damaged cells before they have a chance to become cancerous. Weak brittle nails, dull hair, split ends and many other skin conditions like Acne, Eczema, and Psoriasis can be ameliorated by using this product.

SEXUAL HEALTH

Trace elements in "All Day Energy" are known to increase free testosterone in the blood, which promotes increased libido in both sexes. For men, the high organic content can increase sperm production and maintain good prostate health. Sperm contains 700 times more zinc than is found in blood plasma, and the prostate contains more zinc than any other organ in the body. Low zinc levels can result in prostate swelling, low sperm count, and loss of libido.

WHAT IS GLUTATHIONE?

Glutathione is one of the most important molecules you need present in your body to stay healthy and to prevent disease. It's the body's natural secret ingredient to preventing ageing, cancer, heart disease, dementia and much, much more. Its presence in the body is necessary to treat everything from Alzheimer's to Autism. There have been more than 80,000 medical articles written about it, and it truly is the King of Antioxidants. It is the master of detoxification and the key to a healthy immune system.

Your body produces its own Glutathione naturally. However, things like the "natural ageing process," bad diet, daily ingestion of toxins, medications, and stress all deplete our natural levels of Glutathione. When Glutathione levels become depleted in your body, you can start to encounter unrestrained cell disintegration from things like oxidative stress, free radicals, and infections. The results from this situation is that your liver then gets overloaded with toxins and finds it hard to do its job of detoxification.

When your liver function becomes compromised, your blood quality starts to drop. It becomes sticky and gloopy. This leads to an inability of the blood to deliver fresh oxygen and nutrition to hard working muscles and to provide the nutritional support to repair daily cell damage and slow down the ageing process.

Glutathione can help us reach and sustain our peak mental and physical function. And who would not want that? If you are finding that you could do with more energy, mental focus and are overloaded with daily stress, you likely have Glutathione deficiency.

The Top British medical journal, "The Lancet," found that the highest Glutathione levels occur in healthy young people, while there were substantially lower levels in the elderly and still lower levels of Glutathione in the unwell elderly group, the lowest of all was recorded in the hospitalized elderly.

Keeping yourself fit and healthy, sustaining high physical and mental performance levels, while preventing disease and slowing down the ageing process all depends on keeping your Glutathione levels high. Glutathione is critical for controlling inflammation and maintaining a healthy immune system. It is the master detoxifier and the body's main antioxidant, protecting our cells and making our energy metabolism run well.

#2 SPORTSMAX

SportsMax is a natural cardiovascular supplement suitable for all ages and manufactured in Ireland. It is a mixture of amino acids, L-arginine and L-citrulline, vitamins, minerals, and antioxidants in a powdered drink formulation which has been shown to have positive effects on cardiovascular health and total body wellbeing. When the ingredients in SportsMax are mixed with water and drunk, they combine to produce Nitric Oxide. The science of this formula is based on 30 years of research by Dr. Louis Ignarro, Professor of Pharmacology at UCLA, who received the Nobel Prize for Medicine in 1998 for his work on cardiovascular health. Dr. Ignarro discovered that Nitric Oxide (NO), a molecule produced naturally in the body, is a vasodilator that helps to control the flow of blood to every part of your body. He demonstrated how Nitric Oxide regulates blood flow, prevents blood clots, and protects against vascular plaque or hardening of the arteries as we know it. Combining his own research with fellow scientists in the UK who had studied the mechanism of this Nitric Oxide production, he demonstrated how oral administration of specific amino acids could boost the body's production of Nitric Oxide.

Substantially improving full body circulation leads to better performance, quicker reaction times, and faster recovery times. This is all possible due to the ability of SportsMax to create and then hold Nitric Oxide in your body for an extended period.

Without the production of Nitric Oxide, the lining of an arterial wall becomes very sticky, like Velcro. Then you get a buildup of plaque and debris, which in turn will lead to a decrease in blood flow. When the natural rate of blood flow slows down, you may experience a rise in Blood Pressure and an overall increased level of fatigue. This is as a result of a loss of your ability to efficiently transport oxygen. This loss of oxygen then kills brain and heart cells which can lead to a heart attack or stroke.

SportsMax is designed to help you get the most out of every fitness session, and then it allows you to enjoy the rewards safe in the knowledge that you are getting the maximum health benefits from your efforts.

SportsMax can help you:

- Increase Energy Levels.
- Slow down the Ageing process.
- Reduce Body Fat.
- Recover from Exercise Faster.
- Quicker Reaction Times.
- Better Immune System Function.
- Achieve Greater Endurance Levels.
- Increase circulation.
- Offset the symptoms of Fatigue.
- Improve brain function.

What makes this product different from other Sports Performance Drinks is the incredible list of benefits that can be enjoyed, not just during your sports but for every minute of every day, and they are all available from this proven formula. The fact that you are stimulating the body for optimum performance during exercise as well as repairing the body at the same time, and you can be safe in the knowledge that you are keeping your arteries clear of plaque, stabilizing your blood pressure and lowering your cholesterol levels at the same time is truly amazing. People who exercise should take SportsMax because it will greatly increase your ability to deliver lots more oxygen and vital nutrition to every cell in your body. This is the key factor to improving every system and function in your body that will enhance your performance and speed up your recovery times for sport, work, and life; thus, providing you with the energy to live your life to the max.

These are just two supplements from our range that I recommend for athletes who want to take their energy levels to the next stage. I personally take both of these supplements, and I honestly think you will be happily surprised at the extra energy and well-being you will receive from these nutrition supplements.

For more information about the products

- All Day Energy
- SportsMax
- Brain Power
- Immune Boost
- Stress Repair

Go to: **www.QuantumFlowPerformance.com**

FINAL THOUGHTS

By following the Quantum Flow Running program, you will learn how to get the very best from every training session. You will gain a deeper understanding of the techniques which will teach you the most important skill of all – how to restore and take charge of your own personal health and vitality. As you work through this program, you will find increases in your flexibility and strength and these two key benefits will make running and daily life much easier to enjoy.

When our body is physically tight and restricted, tension is reflected in our mood and thought process. So, as we loosen up and become stronger we become more tolerant, creative, and confident.

Running and exercise should be fun. It is a chance to leave all the stresses of daily life behind, even if it is for just a short while. Knowing that every step you take is bringing you closer to your goal can have a very positive effect on your mood. In fact, it is probably the most instantly rewarding activity that you will undertake on any given day. As you relax into every run, you can be safe in the knowledge that you are either building up much valued energy for the day ahead or letting the stress of another busy day melt away. You are becoming your own psychiatrist and fitness expert all in one go. Running should not be perceived as a chore, but there will be times when you may feel a little less motivated to get up off your sofa and put your runners on. It is on those days you should remind yourself of the proven health benefits that can be gotten from regular exercise and the obvious benefits to your overall well-being.

If you can just take the first few steps, the rest of the workout will look after itself. That is why your warm up sequence is designed to loosen up your body, increase your core temperature, and elevate your heart rate gradually. Once that starts to happen you flood the body and mind with fresh oxygen and release a flood of positive, mood enhancing hormones. You trigger a whole set of chemical reactions in the brain that in turn changes your total physiology.

We need to start looking after our own personal health and educating our friends and family members so that they will not become dependent on others for the state of their vitality as well as their physical and mental health.

I sincerely wish you every success along your path to total health and well-being and hope this book will in some small way inspire you to live a healthier, happier, and more rewarding life. The life you deserve.

AUTHOR BIO

Tony has been practicing Holistic Health Therapies since 1998 including Pilates, CranioSacral Therapy, and Bio-Testing. His goal is to help clients become mentally, physically and emotionally self-sufficient. He has been a running enthusiast for the past 20 years and has decided to combine his holistic health knowledge with his love of running to develop and share a program that is designed to harness and bring the benefits of running into successful daily living. He maintains a private practice in Dublin, Ireland where he lives with his wife and two children.

CONNECT WITH TONY

Website: www.QuantumFlowPerformance.com.

Email: tony@QuantumFlowPerformance.com

Facebook: www.facebook.com/ quantumflowperformance

Twitter: @TheQuantumFlow

Health, Energy & Nutrition Videos

https:/ / quantumflowperformance.com/ pages/ videos

ACKNOWLEDGMENTS

To my good friend and author Alex Clarke who patiently guided me through the writing of this book. Without her direction and input, this book would still be just another document on my laptop.

To Monika Foltman for shooting the Quantum Flow Exercises.

To Una Healy of Una Healy Design for creating the Quantum Flow Running cover.

To Craig Lawless whose behind the scene work on the project has been invaluable.

I would also like to thank my clients who have trusted my methods and taught me so much along the way.

It is very important to acknowledge all the hard work that has gone into research and development over the years by countless coaches and trainers whose findings are the foundation for new advancements in the area of body conditioning and movement.

Special thanks must go to the Aer Lingus Athletics Club, especially my track coach Gerry Martin, my training pals Colm and Eugene who pushed me around the track week after week with no let-up in their focus and humor, and also many thanks to the ALSAA Sports Complex at the Dublin Airport for allowing me to use their facilities.

Printed in Great Britain
by Amazon